Vanishing Village

Vanishing Village

The Struggle for Community in the New West

Evan Blythin

Las Vegas, Nevada

Editor: Geoff Schumacher
Cover Designer: Sue Campbell
Cover Photography: Al Ing
Book Designer: Krissy Hawkins
Production Coordinator: Stacey Fott

First Edition

Library of Congress Cataloging-in-Publication data
Blythin, Evan.
  Vanishing village: the struggle for community in the new West / Evan
Blythin. 202 p. ; 19 cm.
ISBN: 1-935043-19-6 (pbk.)
ISBN: 1-935043-23-4 (ebook)
ISBN-13: 978-1-935043-19-5 (pbk.)
ISBN-13: 978-1-935043-23-2 (ebook)
A look at how a small community, Blue Diamond, Nevada, has handled
community problems in the past thirty years and how the village and its
residents have changed.
1. Blue Diamond (Nev.)—Social life and customs. 2. Communities.
3. Rural Conditions. I. Title.
307.7/2 dc22   2010   2010922787

CITYLIFE
BOOKS

An imprint of Stephens Press, LLC • P.O. Box 1600 (89125-1600)
1111 West Bonanza Road • Las Vegas, Nevada 89106
www.stephenspress.com • www.lvcitylifebooks.com
Printed in United States of America

Foreword

by

GEOFF SCHUMACHER

M y guess is you've never read a book quite like this. Part memoir, part manifesto, *Vanishing Village* is both a portrait of a special place and one man's prescription for a better way of living. It's an intimate look at one speck on the planet and a set of guiding principles for communities across the globe.

What Evan Blythin describes in *Vanishing Village* is a community where everybody knows everybody, and where neighbors look after one another. It's a place where disputes typically are resolved by neighbors, not some distant government body. A place where people respect the land, don't judge one another's predilections, and freely volunteer their time and expertise. It's an enticing alternative to the alienating, impersonal places where so many of us live today.

Blythin's village — a small community outside Las Vegas called Blue Diamond — is not Utopia. There are good people and not-so-good people. They have issues. Some battle personal demons, while others are harmful to the wider community. But the village doesn't ignore its problems or turn to some external authority to solve them.

Personal conflicts, however, are not the village's greatest

challenge. That distinction goes to outside forces. Government entities are constantly trying to impose urban solutions on the rural community, while developers are relentless in their quest to "improve" the village's character through the rapid addition of hundreds or thousands of residents. In both ways, a successful lifestyle is put at risk.

What's most intriguing to me is that Blythin's message is essentially a conservative one. Not conservative in a noxious talk radio way, but conservative as the word is classically defined: protecting something good from the ravages of progress. He's an advocate of "devolution," a repudiation of the failed aspects of modern life. He writes: "I suggest that urbanites surrender before all is lost. There is still time for megalopolis to abandon its evil ways."

Blythin is not a Luddite or an old crank pining for a past that never really was. He wrote this book on a computer. A musician, he distributes his recordings on CDs. He sees the latest movies. He's engaged with what's going on in the world. But he also knows firsthand from his extensive experiences in Blue Diamond that there's another way to live our lives and manage our communities, a viable alternative to America's soul-killing cities and suburbs. *Vanishing Village* belongs on a shelf with books such as Henry David Thoreau's *Walden*, Jane Jacobs' *The Death and Life of Great American Cities*, and Jame Howard Kunstler's *The Geography of Nowhere*.

But please, don't take my word for it. Read this unusual book and judge for yourself.

Geoff Schumacher is the editor of CityLife Books.

Contents

Preface

The village has been an enduring human habitat. I suspect that human society began with a village, a small collection of people living in close proximity, with shared social, economic, political, and belief systems.

But things are changing. The new "global village," for example, is held together by electronic sight and sound, while the village, as I've known it, is held together by flesh and blood.

Housing developers advertise "villages." Their villages are composed of houses that are fronted by garages rather than porches, by living spaces that are isolated from neighbors, in neighborhoods that may offer structured activities but no common goals.

The new, marketed editions of the village illustrate how far we've come from the villages and villas of yesteryear. I live in a village, and I can see that the village of the past is slipping away, vanishing.

Traditionally, village issues have been dealt with in ways that are personal. In the urban environment, issues are dealt with in ways that are impersonal, distant, out of touch. Unfortunately urban encroachment and urban control are changing the village.

The difference between village and urban environments can be seen in the issues they share. The table of contents outlines the issues treated in this book.

The issues are as important in a village as they are in New York City. But my village has addressed them differently than they are addressed in megalopolis. As often as not, I think we have handled them better.

I'd like to tell you about my village.

My Village

To reach my village, you travel through a large desert valley that has been turned into the megalopolis known as Las Vegas. As you move toward the western edge of the valley, you travel through miles of densely populated suburbs. As you leave Las Vegas, you gain altitude and emerge into a smaller, sparsely populated valley. You begin to see natural desert flora and fauna. Ten miles from the edge of Las Vegas, you find yourself at the mouth of a spectacular canyon with red cliffs rising one thousand feet into the sky.

My village is at the mouth of the canyon.

ooo

My village has been here for thousands of years. First it was a tribal village of indigenous peoples hunkered around one of the many springs that flow in this high-desert canyon, living under the shade of ancient willow, cottonwood, and mesquite trees. Then the Spanish came, followed by Anglos who raised cattle and found a valuable mineral deposit on the north hill.

An anthropologist told me that the whole of the Las Vegas Valley, from the mountains to the Colorado River, would have supported five hundred indigenous people living on the natural resources. Now, by importing vast quantities of water, the valley supports two million people. The primary difference, in my mind, is sustainability. The indigenous people lived here for thousands of years. I don't think we can sustain the current population. But I digress.

ooo

My village assumed its current shape about seventy years ago. It started as a mining town complete with a company store, company money, and company houses on good-sized lots surrounding a central park with a meeting hall and a swimming pool.

My wife, Barbara, and I were drawn to its beauty, its distance from the large urban center twenty-five miles away, and the closeness of the native environment. We were part of a migration, one of many families escaping the urban landscape for a more rural setting, like Romans fleeing the decline of empire.

The village is home to a diverse body of souls. Some of those souls are bound together in three-generation family units with relationships that are sorely complex to newcomers. Some of those souls are linked by common occupations. Others are adrift, lost souls.

We are all tied together by proximity, family ties, common needs, and by the fact of being so few. There are about 350 of us — the number changes with guests, drifters, relatives, births, and deaths.

Unlike the electronic and commercial villages that now make up our world, my village is laden with human pathos. There is a lot of interaction here. We touch one another in our daily lives — we relate in ways that may be impossible for those who live in the electronic global village.

When we arrived, the village was in dire straits. The mine had taken care of the yards, the community center, the pool, and the park, but then the mine sold the village to a company that divided things up and sold the individual homes and commercial buildings. Suddenly, like a colony losing its colonial masters, the village was on its own. Things went adrift.

The original house titles required that homeowners pay yearly dues to maintain the park, pool, and community center. By the second or third sale of a home, escrow companies eventually deleted the maintenance clause, and then there wasn't enough money to cover the expenses.

The more expensive community facilities went first. The tile on the pool started falling off and then the pool started to crack.

The trees at the edge of the pool had sent out roots that were cracking and lifting the pavement around the pool.

The charitable organization set up to run the facilities could no longer maintain the physical plant. A rival organization emerged, but it could not do the job either. Half the village could not maintain the facilities for everyone. Everything went to hell.

When we arrived, the county had condemned the facilities. The community center, the pool, and park were in serious disrepair. Worse, the community was divided upon itself.

Religious fanaticism contributed to the divisions. Before we arrived, each Sunday was given to a different religious group in the community hall. Those services kept people focused on a collective need to maintain the facility. The arrangement worked well for a number of years. As a member of any particular church, you could drive into town on your church's village off-Sundays, or you could take a break for a few weeks. If you were generally religious, you could go every week and get exposed to a variety of religious experiences.

But then one group broke away and built its own church. Having the spiritual community divided upon itself contributed to the general decline of village cohesion. There is a form of religious fanaticism that demands singularity — there shall be one God, and, by God, one church. Manifestations of such fanaticism are common in rural America. There are some small towns in Nevada with more churches than the population can reasonably support — but they forge ahead on a shoestring and the faith that they are the chosen ones.

ooo

I'd like to say that Barbara and I rode in on our white horses and saved the day, but that's not the way it happened. Little by little, we found ourselves enmeshed in community affairs. We had a daughter and soon were involved in the parent-teacher organization, and then the charitable association, and then the town Advisory Council.

Barbara and I are both worker bees and we can be depended on to be there, to pull our share of the load. Even more important, we were neutrals in the family and social squabbles of the village and were valuable for our neutrality.

We and some of the other newbies represented a new beginning, a possible link among the various factions. There were common goals that brought us all together: the need to make our grade school serve our children, to get the community facilities into workable shape, to survive together.

I believe that even without the newbies the village would have eventually pulled back together. As it was, the newbies were able to speed things up. It took all of us to recognize our codependency in order to obtain our common goals. But first, the newbies had to be initiated.

Initiation

Becoming part of a community involves initiation. According to *Webster's New Collegiate Dictionary*, an initiation is composed of the ordeals by which a person is made a member of a society. Becoming a member of my village involved a number of ordeals.

My wife and I were unlikely candidates for village citizenship. We were academics in a community of miners. I had two redeeming talents that gained me relatively quick entrance to village life: I had rural roots and a valuable rural talent — tree topping.

Thirty years ago, when I was a much younger man, I could climb almost any tree, was unafraid of heights, and knew how to trim a tree. The indigenous trees and the trees planted by the early village occupants had obtained considerable height, and many of the houses had become threatened by dropping limbs.

Everyone kept their distance when my wife and I first arrived — we were aliens — until I removed my first tree. Our yard had seven large trees, not groomed and dangerous. By the time I had the second tree out, I had an audience. After high-trimming the remaining trees, I had requests. Over the next two or three years, I trimmed somewhere around thirty large elm trees.

Having demonstrated a work ethic, talent, and willingness to share, characteristics appreciated by the village population, Barbara and I moved toward village acceptance. It also turns out that our academic credentials served village needs.

At first our academic backgrounds were viewed with suspicion — we were university professors. It was as if we had a different smell, and the other beasts suspected we might not be trustworthy. The miners harbored a wariness of pointy-headed academics. In some parts of the world, people who wore glasses were eliminated because the glasses proved they were readers. Everyone knows that intellectuals will almost always sell out the working class. Fortunately, in my village people took their time in assessing newness and sniffed around long enough to find out that education can be a good thing.

One night, as I was busy working on a technical monograph, there was a knock at my study door; it was one of the village miners. The miner knocking at my door and I were very different. He was a giant of a man, about six feet five inches tall and 350 pounds. I am tall but skinny; I could hide behind him.

As different as we were, at first glance we also found common ground. He was a master of an ancient trade and so was I. He worked the minefield, and I worked the field of rhetoric.

The village miner and I drank together and we worked together on community projects. The night he showed up at my study door he had a legal document that needed reading and response. "I wondered if you'd take a look at this and tell me what it means," he said.

The miner had mined the earth for most of his life; he was an expert in a dangerous and laborious field. He knew how to read a slope and how to take down a hill to get to the ore, and do it without killing himself or anyone else. He could drive a hundred-ton loader with a precision nothing short of artful. I appreciated his talents, and he was asking for mine. And I gave them. We became good friends.

Word spread. Soon, my wife and I became the village scribes. Barbara had scored something like ninety-six percent on the national Graduate Record Exams (verbal) and has a graduate degree in math — she's far more dangerous than I am. But she shares her knowledge freely and does not put on airs.

Over the years we have used our talents to augment the lives of our village friends and they have given back ten-fold. When we built our new villa, the heavy equipment and its operation came as a gift from our village friends.

ooo

I think one reason I was able to overcome village distrust of higher education is that I share the distrust. I see every state college striving for university status and faculty members writing monographs at a frenzied pace, leaving undergraduate students to the ministrations of graduate students and underpaid adjuncts.

I see the public cost of all those faculty members thinking they are Aristotle, when in sober fact most of them are low-level scribes cranking out drivel. Mao may have been right: Many university professors could benefit from a little time picking worms in fields of lettuce. I feel strongly enough about the matter to have published an unpopular article regarding the publish-or-perish syndrome in *The Chronicle of Higher Education*.

Eventually I retired from the university. I had kept up with my share of research and publication but I could see that higher education had forsaken its primary mission: the education of our young. I miss the students, but I don't miss the scribblers. I've found the miners to be far wiser and more intellectually challenging than the university crowd.

And so, little by little, we made ourselves at home in the village. We became initiated.

ooo

Our initiation began before we had even moved in. We bought our house through a series of bids in an estate sale. George and

Ruby had been the first occupants of the house and had lived there for almost forty years.

George drove a haul truck at the mine. Ruby made the home as comfortable as possible; the end tables were personalized with hand-made doilies; the furniture was comfortable. Ruby also gardened, and the yard was an oasis of rose bushes, asparagus ferns, and sweet peas. He died, and then she died. And then we bought the house and found ourselves facing a tough initiation.

In traditional indigenous American villages, the other tribe's horses were fair game. Our village retains a touch of tribal ethos. The first things I moved to our new home were tools for home repairs and carvings that I had been working on for eight years. One day I brought in a six-foot elm wood sculpture of Socrates. The next day it was gone.

I asked around but no one knew anything. Years later, I found out who had stolen the work, but by then it didn't matter. I had about one hundred hours in the sculpture, and its loss was a blow. But as Socrates would have said, at least I didn't have thieving on my conscience. It was sort of flattering, having someone risk their integrity and reputation for a piece of my art.

The theft made it clear that I was not a member of the village. I believe that the village harbored a residual tribal attitude toward strangers — the horses of strangers are there for the taking. Until you've been initiated, you are homeless in the village, a stranger.

Strangers are to be approached cautiously and are often treated as objects. For example, I had a friend once who was selling a car and did not want to sell it to a neighbor because he would feel obliged to tell the whole truth about the car. He would get more money from a stranger.

I think the village has changed its phobia regarding strangers. As more and more strangers have moved in, we have become more sensitive to other tribes, other cultures, other sexual preferences, other religions.

We're still suspicious of what Barbara calls "touroids," strangers gawking at our village. But when we first arrived in the village, we were strangers in the tribal sense. Someone had at us. Fortunately, I was busy with the house and did not have the time to get up a posse and hunt down the stealer.

ooo

One day, as I was working on the house, a cocky bull of a man pulled up in front of the driveway, introduced himself, and congratulated me on winning the house in the auction bidding. He was a good-looking man about ten years older than me. He and his wife had been our primary opponents in the bidding.

For his whole life, this soon-to-be-friend had operated and owned heavy equipment. He and his wife moved into the village just before we did; they had seniority. But we, outsiders, beat them at the bidding. Our relationship began as competitors.

We had not met during the written bid process. When our

opponent pulled up to the house, I had no idea who he was. He introduced himself, and after congratulating me on having won the bid, he mentioned that he owned the lot behind the house.

"Would you be interested in buying that back lot?" he asked. I salivated over the thought of having the back lot. I expressed my interest. He read me like a card, and told me that if he ever decided to sell it, I would be the first one he would talk to. Then he drove off.

At the time of his visit, we were not yet in the house. But by virtue of having bid against each other and of having adjacent properties, we were already up close and personal. His visit was a sort of taunt: He had something I wanted, the back lot. But then again, I had something that he wanted, the house. The question was, which of us would end up with both properties?

We dickered and bickered for eight years before Barbara and I finally sold our home to his son. By that time he, his son, and I had gotten to sort of like one another. We'd have a few beers and argue over just about everything. Despite our many differences, we found that we had a lot in common and became very good friends. I wanted more space, found it, and his son bought our house. Everyone ended up happy.

ooo

Our opponent's son had lived next to us when we moved in. He is a lot like his father, up close and personal in every aspect of his life. One day he came by on his way to the local dump. His truck was loaded with junk, and he wanted to know if I had anything I wanted to throw away. I didn't, but while talking I noticed that he had some neat-looking brake drums in his truck. I'm always looking for possible sculpture bases.

"Are you throwing those brake drums?" I asked.

"Oh no," he said, "I'm saving those."

Right, and pigs fly. Desire drives value and he, like his father with the back lot, was very much aware of my desire. I've got to get better at hiding my desires.

The son had not thought of his brake drums as valuable, but once I revealed interest, he needed time to rethink. He went to the dump, but when I went to the dump later in the day, there were no brake drums on his pile of refuse.

Years ago we had our own dump and it was pleasure for us all. I'd take up a load of my junk and come back with somebody else's junk. We really enjoyed one another's junk. There was one junk truck that was moved all over the village before someone got busy and brought it back to life — it was good junk. It was sort of like a moveable sculpture.

We eventually lost our dump because some urban industries started dumping barrels of suspicious oils there. At that point, we were made part of the urban collection service. We lost a valuable village resource.

Anyway, the brake drums were not at the dump. About three weeks later, the brake drums showed up in my driveway. The son later told me, over the fence, that he had extra brake drums and had left a pair for me. He became a close friend, though later we were to be separated by a sad series of events.

I suppose much of this is petty, but pettiness is a part of human nature. In the city, I might never have engaged in the closeness I have with my village neighbors. I would not have come to realize that I have my share of pettiness and that part of friendship is getting beyond pettiness to the heart of the matter.

ooo

Living in the village has placed us in contact with everyone who lives here. None of us knows everyone really well, but all of us know everyone well enough to determine a villager from a touroid.

Community Service

One way that we meet each other, and one form of initiation, is community service. Much like the old ways, where a young person would be initiated to the hunt, the newcomer to the village has traditionally been assimilated on the basis of contribution to the community. Increasingly, community service has been declining in the village. I lay the blame on urban sensitivities.

Before I moved to the village, I had no real concept of community service. Indeed, much to my regret, I was once quite flippant about community service. Many years ago, one of my brightest graduate students was talking about her favorite community service organization. I called the group a bunch of Girl Scouts pushing cookies. I count that as a low spot in my humanness. Living in the village has taught me that other people exist well beyond the virtual level. We are flesh and blood, and we are related.

The village has a number of formal and informal nonprofit organizations that help keep things running. The volunteer fire department takes care of safety issues. The charitable association takes care of the community center, meeting hall, and village park. The county Advisory Council deals with zoning, land use, the county park, and legal compliance with county laws and regulations. The history society searches for and guards our past.

We also have less-structured organizations. The Bunco Bitches is a group of women who gather at various homes for a fun and information-sharing evening. Men are not particularly welcome, so I can only report rumor as to their discussions. I do know that they are a powerful force in terms of spreading information throughout the village. Our women are almost as gossipy as us men.

Men don't attend Bunco Bitch meetings. The same is true of the Red Hats, a loose association of female village elders. They meet in front of the store or wherever they feel like meeting, for morning coffee. A few years ago they all took a trip to a brothel, just checking things out. Like the Bunco Bitches, the Red Hats are often a formidable part of village life.

Community service is the backbone of the village. But the meaning of community service has diminished as more and more urbanites have moved to the village, urbanites who are not conditioned to work for community.

ooo

I suspect that large urban units lack community in part because individuals are alienated from one another and simply do not have a sense of community service. In the cities, people pay their taxes and expect the government to do, well, just about everything.

Nowadays, it seems that most community service is being done by people wearing demeaning outfits doing demeaning work. The village, because of its various volunteer and charitable organizations, is allowed to use community service workers from town, people who broke the law and are punished with community service. They show up surly, pissed off, and totally into the notion that community service is a punishment.

I am one of the villagers who run the punitive community service programs. I view the running of the program as another form of community service, a form that serves both the village and those who have been assigned to the work gang.

I start by sitting down with the workers, with a cup of coffee, and explain that I am grateful for their help and that there are some things that really need to be done. Sometimes those things are menial, but they need to be done, and I don't ask anyone to do what I won't do.

Then I ask about their relative skills and try to match them with work they know. I also work them on a flat-rate basis, just the way my mechanic bills me. I look at a job with the potential worker, and we estimate the time it will take to do the job; that's how much time I give.

I help start the job and then I go away. I tell the worker that if the work is done sooner than my estimate, the flat rate hours are what I count, unless some complication emerges and more hours are required. Sometimes if a community service worker has certain tools or skills, I will count those tools and skills as part of the hour count.

We have had several community service prisoners who did not buy into the notion that the work needed to be done. For instance, I met one worker down at the store, bought him a cup of coffee, and lined him out on the basketball court, which was covered with a layer of leaves and dirt from recent construction activities. I gave him a shovel, rake, and broom, flat-rated the work at two hours, and headed off for other work.

An hour later, I went by the court and found the guy leaning on his broom with no work done. I asked if he was okay, and he said everything was fine except for having to do a shit job. I told him that I thought the job was as significant as any other, and that it needed to be done. Besides, his choices were to service the community, pay some exorbitant fine or do jail time. It seemed to me that cleaning a basketball court on a nice warm, summer day was more pleasure than pain. And I went back to my work.

An hour later, I came back and nothing had been done. I packed up the tools and walked. I've had the same problem with some of the new village people who show up for a community activity and find that the activity requires some physical work. Viewing work as infra-dig, and viewing service as demeaning, diminishes and poses threats to our sense of community.

ooo

The fire department is the most valuable community service in the village. Most old mining towns had volunteer fire departments composed of rudimentary equipment and dedicated personnel. Many of the miners who lived in the village had come here from larger mining towns and had seen some hellacious fires.

One of my village friends, a miner who was many years older than me, told me the story of a fire in Pioche, an old hard-rock mining town in east-central Nevada. Pioche is a marvelous Old West town. In its heyday, Pioche had 15,000 miners working shafts 1,600 feet deep.

My friend had worked for the Pioche mine and had also worked as an independent contractor. The miners would dig down, following the ore. When they found a particularly rich collection, they would make a large chamber supported by twenty- to thirty-foot columns.

When the mine was finished, my friend would contract for the columns. He and his partner would shore up the ceiling with 12x12 timbers and dynamite the columns. They would go down 1,600 feet into the earth and collect the blasted columns. The ceiling beams would have so much pressure that they would go from twelve to eight inches thick. Imagine doing that.

He told me that during the fire, the department enlisted anyone who could carry a bucket — men, women, and children. They stood side by side, in a one hundred-foot line, passing buckets of water from hand to hand, in the face of a fire that was hotter than the hubs of hell. Once in a while, a gallon bottle of whiskey was passed down the line — a fortifier, an ash solvent, a spirit-feeder.

In one fire, they lost the whole town. The town was rebuilt, but on a lesser scale. The mine was petering out and the miners were beginning to look elsewhere. Some of them came to the village.

The village's volunteer fire department has gone through some incredible changes in the past thirty years. There was a time when we would get a call for a wildland fire, and we would load up the outdated fire tenders, stop by the store for a few cases of beer, and go get that sucker. Things have changed.

In my ten years with the fire department, I saw a gradual change in emphasis from fire to roadside emergencies. The county was not too interested in giving us state-of-the-art fire equipment because the village is so small and does not warrant city-scale equipment. But the county was interested in giving us what we needed to deal with accidents on ever-busier roadways.

My last night on the fire department started when my neighbor's father had a heart attack. The victim died, and one of our paramedics brought him back to life. The victim was airlifted to town and did not make it. His demise started around 10:30 p.m., and our assistance was complete somewhere around 12:30 a.m.

About half an hour later, just as I got back to sleep, the phone rang and I was off to a car accident. The victims were mine workers, good looking, young, hard-working people. We think they were moving along at an exhilarating pace. They missed a curve and were torn apart by the very mountain that had given them sustenance.

I got home about 5 a.m., just about time to shower and go to work. Then I quit the department. In my ten years on the fire department, I got a chance to see the volunteer spirit that exists in volunteer fire departments all over the country. Urban folks have no concept of the sacrifices and images endured by volunteer firefighters.

There was one emergency call that I missed, and I'm glad. A man on the other side of the village had been through a long, painful battle with cancer. One night he put an end to endless pain. He used a large-bore handgun. His wife found him in a scene that must have haunted her for the rest of her life. Our guys got the call.

There is no way to reverse such calamities. They are beyond salvage. But there are rituals. There is holding the wounded one, there is letting the tears run down your shoulder. There is pain-sharing. Our folks did all of that and more.

As I understand the situation, our guys got the wife away from the immediate scene, made all the appropriate formal contacts. The widow had help through the night, she had people she knew, people who understood the depth of her loss.

ooo

I can't talk about the volunteer fire department without talking about its enduring life forces. Our fire chief is a professional who has been very busy and successful. For more than twenty years he has dedicated himself to the volunteer fire department. He has brought the village into the twenty-first century.

Our chief is a big, good-looking man. He is very persuasive, and he has persuaded the county that we are worthy of some largess. He has seen a cadre of people and himself through advanced fire and safety training. He has helped give the village a body of trained paramedics.

I believe that for a village to survive, the villains and the inhabitants of the villas must work together. Our chief has a nice villa, and no one begrudges his success because he has shared it with us all. May the Maker bless him.

Our chief has been a prime mover in the fire department, and he has attracted a lot of talent. He has helped train several of our young people for lifetimes of valuable work. We have a village couple who both work hard jobs, and yet have dedicated more than twenty years of their life to make the fire department work. The newcomers don't seem quite willing to make such a commitment.

ooo

Volunteer firefighters are given a great deal of respect in rural areas. I got the benefit of that respect in one of my outback trips when I was on the department.

I was in upper Nevada on what is called "The Loneliest Highway in America." I was doing 105 miles per hour. The tall brush at the edge of the road was whipping by like a solid gray-green fence. It was beautiful, open desert valley country, one long expanse after another. I was having a good time.

Then I crested the fateful hill and drove right into the radar scope of the highway patrolman standing at his car door. He had me cold. I hit the brakes and pulled in right next to his car.

He walked up to the window and did the cop thing — license, insurance, and so forth. He ran my plates, he checked the equipment, he eyeballed everything he could see in my vehicle. He noticed my fire department badge on the dash.

He held his ticket book in his hand while he took a long look at the badge. "What do you do?" he asked, pointing to the badge.

"I clean the fire station, check the equipment, do fire and road calls, drive the trucks, and do what is needed," I told him.

He told me that my speed could result in confiscation of my vehicle, a jail cell, and extensive legal maneuvering. He also told me he thought that maybe his scope might have been wrong but he knew I had been going at least 85 miles per hour and would swear to it in court.

I agreed with his assessment and took my ticket like a man.

ooo

Unfortunately, much of the funding for volunteer fire departments comes from the urban centers. Often those centers are resentful of small rural areas sucking on urban dollars. What those city folks fail to realize is that villages help sustain urban centers.

My village has supplied minerals to the larger population and takes care of urban tourists. Other villages supply food. I view the village as a primary human resource, a core of human activity, one that survives on the backs of volunteers, people who act beyond a salaried position, people who care about the other people who live around them.

ooo

A number of years ago, a second-generation miner passed away. He had been raised here, he raised his family here, he was a decent man. He died here. This miner was a really big man. When he went to work at the mine, his lunchbox was a large cooler. He was said to be able to put away two chickens, at least a loaf of bread, and some miscellaneous dessert items at one sitting. The really neat thing about this miner was that he was incredibly decent. As big as he was, he never tried to bully anyone. He didn't try to manage everyone else's life, but he ran his life by a strict code of behavior.

When the miner died, his family was left in a momentary financial fix. He had reasonable life insurance and his wife worked, but the insurance company paid slowly. The guys in the fire department fired up the trucks and made a complete sweep of the village. Enough money was raised to get the family past the financial crisis.

One of the miner's daughters became a volunteer firefighter, went through all the formal training expected of professional firefighters, became a paramedic, and ultimately became a registered nurse. That's the way we'd like for things to work out in the village.

ooo

Our chief has welcomed a number of young people to the fire department. While some don't follow through, the occasional success is gratifying.

One of our young men joined the department when he was a teenager. He showed great aptitude in his service to the volunteer fire department. He was not afraid to work, and he was not afraid of the county training and tests. He worked his way through just about every certification possible and ultimately applied for a job with a professional fire department.

He passed the test with flying colors, and now, at a very young age, has high seniority in his fire department. I don't think that urban fire departments embrace the youth of their communities the way they are embraced in the village.

ooo

Much of the community service that takes place in the village is for the health of the village in general. We gather together to maintain community assets. But as I've indicated, we also take care of one another on personal levels. Years ago, I was the beneficiary of village largess while teaching in Northern Spain.

Barbara was in the middle of her graduate work on a degree in mathematics, was working under a scholarship, and could not accompany me. So I left her, a teenager, two dogs, and two cats, and I went to Spain. She's never quite forgiven me for that trip.

But everything worked out fine. I wasn't her only support; she had the village on her side. When the water heater went out, a village friend took care of the matter.

While gone, the village looked after my family. It also continued to pay attention to me. One day, about the middle of my stay, I received a package from the village, a half-gallon of peanut butter.

The package had $50 worth of stamps on it. My landlady was a stamp collector and wanted to know if she could have the stamps. No problema.

But what really knocked her socks off was the peanut butter. Apparently peanut butter had not oozed its way to Northern Spain. I trucked down to the local market to buy crackers, and introduced my landlady to the joys of peanut butter.

Then I took the jar to school and introduced the faculty to peanut butter. I treated the janitor to some crackers with peanut butter. I was quite the hit. I've worked hard to take care of the village, and it has worked hard to take care of me, helping me bring good cheer to Northern Spain.

Recreation

How people play is an important part of urban and suburban planning. In the village, we play according to seasonal tradition and village inclination.

Our most popular seasonal party is the fall festival. The festival began years ago as the "deer hunters' ball." The hunters in the village would return with venison, and there would be a blow-out party. A rifle would be raffled, and money would be raised for community projects.

The festival was generally a rowdy affair, replete with dancing, drinking, feasting, and fighting. When my wife and I showed up, the deer hunters' ball had evolved into a fall festival centered on a pit-cooked pig.

The festival was a week-long event that started with the digging of a six-by-eight-foot hole about five feet deep. For several days, we brought in large pieces of wood to fill the hole, the pig was butchered, and the women started working on salads, side dishes, and desserts.

For about twenty-five years one of our village friends was the chef. Not only did he know how to pit-cook a pig, he knew the fine art of Dutch-oven cooking, could barbecue with the best, and was a killer cook with beans. He could feed hundreds of people.

Two days before the festival, the men would gather in the evening and start the fire. It was quite a blaze and the center of village attention. The men would gather and drink, argue, gossip, do business, and make trades. Some of the younger guys would drink a bit too much. Once in a while, someone would fall into the burning pit. That was always exciting.

The next day, more wood would be added. By the evening or the following morning, the bottom of the pit would be lined with a layer of very hot coals. The pig would get stuffed with a variety of stuffings and wrapped in wet burlap, tinfoil, and chicken wire. A few vent pipes would be placed into the hole, the pig would be lowered into the pit and covered with a layer of dirt. My description of the pig cook is rough, an amateur's view of the art.

When the pig came out of the hole, the chief pig cooker, with four or five helpers, would start the slicing and dicing. First the head was removed. A beer would be installed into the mouth, and the head was passed around for a shared drink. The women avoided the ceremony and the kids would go out and puke in the bushes.

Then the party would begin. The whole community would show up, and a long line would form along the tables heaped with home-cooked side dishes, salads, and desserts. It was an incredibly good feast. There was a nominal fee to help cover the expenses of the community center.

After the meal, everyone engaged in a short but intense auction of donated items. Then some tables would be removed, the band would start, and the dancing would commence.

ooo

In those years we could count on at least two or three fights in the course of an evening, mostly drunken brawls that resulted in a few bruised egos, a lot of grunting and groaning and, once in a while, a solidly landed blow.

One year, a villager's relative got totally drunk and fell off a bar stool, onto the floor, and into a puddle of beer and urine. Some of the village folks packed him out and into the back of his friend's pickup. An hour or so later, the friend decided to leave. He looked for his friend, could not find him, and took off for home. His place was a few miles down the paved road, and then about five miles of really rough dirt road. He hauled ass down the bumpy road, went to bed, and got a good night's rest.

The next morning, the beaten and battered friend staggered out of the truckbed and stumbled through the front door. He was black and blue and bloody all over. He had bounced around in the back of the pickup until every part of his body had suffered. He thought someone had beaten him up, and he was not happy about it.

The village relative finally figured it out. The friend told another friend who told someone in the village and pretty soon the story became part of village legend.

There are other legends originating at the fall festival, some great music, some interesting liaisons, some good trades, and so forth. I don't think they do this kind of stuff in the city.

Now we have a well-engineered brick-lined pit, with a spring-loaded steel top. Our parties are fun, but more moderate — I suppose you could say we've become more urbane, perhaps more civilized. And yet, we're retained a strong sense of community recreation. We party together, we get a little loose, we dance and sing.

ooo

It has been thirty years since my first pig cook and the affair has gone through a lot of changes. We no longer dig holes and use five cords of firewood to cook a pig — we've built a vault and have moved to a pit system that uses lava rock heated by the fire to cook whatever we want to cook.

We no longer spend a week getting ready for the pig. We don't stand around the fire and drink like we used to. We gather in the very early morning before the sun rises and get the pit fired.

We have the pig or turkeys or brisket, whatever, in the pit by around midday. By evening we are eating.

The process of the fall festival has changed, but the tradition remains and it still takes a large number of community members to make the party work. We haven't had a fight in a number of years, and arguers are taken outside and isolated until they are willing to come back into the community hall and join the party.

They don't do fund-raising fall festivals in suburban subdivisions, not where residents throw their own party. Downtown, they do catering; they gather together as anonymous residents attending an institutional gathering. Those poor suckers don't know what they are missing.

ooo

When we first moved here, the village sport was horseshoes. We started out with a few pits and ultimately developed twenty-four professional horseshoe pits. We competed with one another, and we competed with outlying communities. We ran a May tournament that would draw as many as one hundred shooters.

A village couple who owned the village market sponsored competitive horseshoe tournaments. They helped develop extra pits in the community park, and they built pits on the store property. They threw a good tournament and had competitors from as far away as Oklahoma.

We had some pretty good players. The village fox, a very shrewd and precise man, threw a beautiful side-turning shoe that was marvelous to watch. Spinning sideways, the heel of his shoe would catch on the post and spin around it like something that had a life of its own. One of my best village friends and his sons were hard to beat. They threw shoes that flipped and would fall on the post in a flat and decisive way.

For several years, we had a national champion who came to our tournament just to kick our butts and take our money. I never knew his last name, but he was a real sharpshooter. He also made great and strong beer and would share with his horseshoe competitors. He would beat a lot of our young guys with his excellent malt beverages, but we ultimately beat him with our women.

We tend to not be sexist in the village and pride ourselves on our competent women. Sometimes we think they may be smarter than us men. It was only natural that some of the women would want to compete in the horseshoe tournaments.

The women pressed to play against the men, and we men agreed. Playing by international rules, we found ourselves getting regularly bested. So it was that one year the out-of-town sharpshooter showed up and found women in the sport. He thought that was really funny.

He found himself, in the final round, pitching shoes against two village women. He laughed and opened another of his fine beers.

Our women had a few of his beers, and showed him how horseshoes should be thrown. They threw one of the best games I have ever seen, one ringer after another. They had a good time. He, on the other hand, had been a gloating winner, and he was a terrible loser.

Everyone was there for the big game. He used to taunt the people he was beating. As he and his partner began to lose their game with our women, he began to take some serious payback from his audience.

"Maybe you should try the C level," someone suggested.

"Or," someone suggested, "maybe shoot with the kids."

It was pretty humiliating stuff and eventually some in the audience got around to his very manhood. In old-speak, he left town with his tail between his legs. We never saw him again.

ooo

The Greeks had games. So did the Romans, the Medievals, and the Moderns. Contemporary urban units still have games, but they have become remote from particular communities and more people have become viewers instead of participants. It's gotten to resemble the games of overpopulated falling Rome.

State universities maintain competitive sports, but their teams are composed of mercenaries, not local product. On the professional level, we have the Los Angeles Rams playing in St. Louis and the Oakland Raiders playing in Los Angeles, and then back to Oakland. I suppose it really doesn't matter since the

Los Angeles Rams are not made up of players from Los Angeles and the Oakland Raiders are not from Oakland.

The village still runs a May horseshoe tournament. We entertain ourselves. In the village, our entertainment is personal.

ooo

There has never been a licensed bar, tavern, or saloon in the village. People here have never wanted a drinking establishment because of the problems associated with such a business. But that doesn't mean we don't drink or party.

The village market used to sell packaged hard liquor and continues to sell beer and wine. Drinking has always taken place at individual homes, at parties thrown in the community hall, and in the community park.

When I first moved here, the miners would come home from a hard day and stop by the park for a drink or two under a large cottonwood tree. On Friday and Saturday nights, people would get together, drink and sometimes crawl home. In some ways, it was like Europe where neighborhood drinking establishments take care of the locals and no one has to drive.

Yes, once in a while, someone would get carried away, and there would be some yelling and high good times. Once in a while someone would get so shit-faced they'd puke all the way home, and the kids would get to see firsthand what booze can do.

I made myself at home. It was nice to come home after a hard day of academic BS and wander down to the park for a drink and an exchange of the latest news. It also was an opportunity to buy, sell, trade, and work out community problems. On Saturdays we all enjoyed a little over-indulgence to wash out the taste of a difficult week.

On Saturday evenings, some people show up with musical instruments and we sing and dance, hoot and holler. As in inner-city streets, the original "tree bar" had a burn barrel. Even in the coldest part of the winter, we'd party together.

It was primitive, but it worked. And then there was a sea change that led to a more civilized environmental tree bar.

ooo

The pretty woman moved here from town, leased a house above the park and lived there for a year before buying the house. I suspect that while renting a house, she didn't feel she had the right to complain about the drinking and noise coming from the park. Once she became a homeowner, though, she started complaining.

She came to those of us doing much of the partying and asked us to tone it down. She was right, we did get out of hand. We had an all-trash-can band that could wake up the dead. We had one big miner who could bellow and buffalo would fall to their knees. We sang loudly and often badly. Some arguments progressed to high decibel levels.

But we did not take her complaints too seriously, in part because everyone had to wonder why she would buy a house knowing she did not like the behaviors of her neighbors. There is a resentment against newcomers who immediately try to change village life.

But she was a tough person and so she persisted. She went to the association that manages the park and demanded a stop to the raucous recreating going on at the tree bar. The association heard her out and explained that the people she was complaining about were her neighbors and the very people who served on the volunteer fire department, who maintained the five-acre park, the community center, the pool, and who were all members of the association. She didn't like that.

She appealed to county authorities but found that our activities were legal. We gave her points for persistence and took her objections seriously enough to deal with some of the noise and aesthetic objections.

No one retaliated against the newbie challenging village tradition. But the village tradition did change by virtue of the challenge. We formalized our place in the universe by creating the Tree Bar.

We selected a spot on the edge of the park that faced the village market and we dug in. We brought in truckloads of dirt and made a berm that insulated us from the houses on the upper road (where the woman lived).

We put a nice roof over the area, supported by posts and beams made from telephone poles. Then we added a nice mortared rock floor. We partied on, but we brought it down a few notches. About half the village shows up at different times throughout the year to play and listen to music that we make.

Mexican villages have their central parks and bands that play on the weekend. In Europe, most small villages and towns have formal outdoor areas for music and recreation. The new lady moved us up, helped civilize us.

I suppose you could say that the new woman was initiated, she made her bones, she made a valuable contribution to the village. Now, about ten years after the initial battles, the Tree Bar has become an international symbol of village social life. Over the years, all sorts of add-ons have happened so that one protruding rafter has an airplane propeller on it, and the cross beams are covered with interesting artifacts from around the world — license plates, old toys, weird signs, and so forth.

Every Saturday night, local musicians and their friends gather for an evening of some pretty good music. Last week we had a clarinet, a stand-up bass, a violin, several guitars, a xylophone, and various rhythm instruments. Sometimes we sound really good.

Busloads of tourists show up at the village market and a million pictures have been taken of the Tree Bar. A year or so ago, we received a copy of a Japanese newspaper that featured a picture of the Tree Bar. People from around the world have posted letters to the Tree Bar, which the village post office forwards to a mailbox in front of the Tree Bar. There is something primal about a community center where friends and neighbors can gather — a people's park.

When I see subdivisions advertised as villages, I am highly skeptical. Community is built by community. We maintain our own swimming pool, our community center, our park, and our Tree Bar. If those advertised subdivisions were true villages, they would be built with a vacant center and the community would create and maintain what it wanted, which is not always a golf course or gym.

ooo

A lot of village business gets taken care of at the Tree Bar. A lot of goofing off also occurs. One day, there were about ten of us at the Tree Bar and I was cutting up some fresh habanero chilies from my garden, passing around tastes of the hottest peppers I'd even grown.

One of our young guys showed up, watched for a while, and finally observed that I was sure cutting the peppers into small pieces. "What a bunch of wussies," was his exact sentiment. He had tried various chilies in his young life and thought that jalapenos were the hottest. Everyone else knew better. One thing led to another and the challenge was made — let's see you eat a whole habanero.

No problema, he said.

He popped the habanero into his mouth, gave a few chews, and swallowed. He had our full attention. He broke out in a sweat and his face went red. He quaffed a beer or two, which did not help at all. Then his breathing became ragged and he was clearly in acute pain. For a while there, we thought he was going to pass out.

We enjoyed the hell out of that. As my friend Mike says, "Young men think old men are stupid — old men know that young men are." Of course that can work the other way. As we all know, "There's no fool like an old fool."

ooo

Village recreation often takes rural forms. Pit-cooked pigs, horseshoes, tree bars, and hot peppers all reflect the rural influence in village recreation. One of the more interesting recreations, pumpkin growing, was quite the rage for a few years.

It started in 1990, with news of a Northman who grew a 612-pound pumpkin. Wayne came up with the thought of a village contest for the biggest pumpkin. I bought the seed. Terry said he was going to hollow his out, polish it up, and make it into a spare room. I planned on putting wheels on mine and using it for a trailer.

The contest ended up with twelve participants. The whole village watched with bated breath. Some people never got their seeds in the ground. Some people lost their plants before bearing fruit. Two people did remarkably well.

55

Don has a green thumb, and he produced the biggest pumpkins. He had eight pumpkins in the seventy- to eighty-pound range. But even such large pumpkins did not win the prize.

The prize went to Guy. He had a 104-pound monster. There was talk of another contest but many people were intimidated by Don and Guy.

In 1993, the contest continued with seven serious pumpkin growers. This time, the contest had a $25 entry fee. The winner was to get sixty percent, second place would get twenty percent, and third place got fourteen percent. I ended up with a 64-pound pumpkin, Cecil had a 41-pounder, and Guy had a 28-pounder. But that was not the end of the fun.

In 1994, Cecil (the fox) made a run to the front and finished the race. Cecil is challenged rather than beaten by defeat. He has been one of the master gardeners in the village and was not about to be bested in growing something as a basic as a squash.

He read the books, he called the seed companies, he stayed up late swallowing information and planning his victory. He started in the fall, with a giant hole filled with the best pumpkin fodder. He planted after the last frost, with seeds transported from the land of the midnight sun where they grow pumpkins up to 940 pounds big.

He built wind breaks to protect the sail-like leaves. As the plants grew, he extended his water lines so the main vines could tap into the ground and add to their available supply of water and nutrients.

His whole back yard was filled with pumpkin vines, and he watched them with all the concern of a patient mother. He couldn't leave the village very often. When he did, he abused his loved ones and friends with detailed orders on the feeding and watering of his babies.

Cecil's pumpkin was 157 pounds. Guy came in with a 75-pound monster, and I came in last with a 45-pound lightweight. It was a good year. And it was the last year of the giant pumpkin contest. Cecil killed us with a record that probably never will be matched in the village. Cecil the fox.

ooo

We party together in the village. Our fall festival, our horseshoe tournament, our Tree Bar, our pumpkin contests are all examples of how a community can entertain itself. I don't see urban or suburban communities entertaining themselves. I look downtown, and I see large anonymous audiences for sport or music, but I don't see people getting together in community recreation. That's sad.

The Tree Bar

At first glance the Tree Bar is a unique recreational hangout. It was built using telephone poles with traditional post-and-beam construction and a corrugated tin roof. The back and side walls were made from telephone poles dug in like the walls of old Southwestern forts. Odds and ends are hung on the poles and nailed along the four-foot-high walls. The structure sits under a small grove of cottonwood trees. It's an entertaining and functional structure.

Sometimes people stop because they think the Tree Bar is a public or commercial recreational facility. For some in the village, the Tree Bar is strictly a recreational asset, a place to drop by for a drink, for some music, or for the warmth of the stove on a cold afternoon.

From many perspectives the Tree Bar is recreational, but it goes much deeper than that. The Tree Bar is as important as the post office, the market, the church, the charitable association, and the Advisory Council. Every community should have a Tree Bar.

At its most basic level, the Tree Bar is a gathering of people — people who drink, sing, argue, and deal with community issues. The patrons are also the leaders or members of the charitable association, the fire department, the Advisory Council, and most of the other community organizations.

There are some deep resentments against the Tree Bar. The biggest is the drinking. For some people, alcohol is a horrible drug. Indeed, alcohol has destroyed many lives. It is a resentment that I understand very well. My mother was an orphan by virtue of a drunk-driving father. She knew the negative effects of alcohol and by golly the rest of the family had better adhere to her rule of no alcohol. She is in her nineties now, and holds steady to her aversion to drinking. So we all had to sneak to get a drink.

Pop would sneak out to the barn, where he kept a well-stocked refrigerator. When I got up to my thirties and would visit the ranch, Pop and I snuck out together, to the barn, to the cold beer. We never got drunk together, but we loosened up with each other and some of the best moments of my life were sitting out in the barn, keeping an eye out for Mom, having a cold beer on a hot day.

My mother knew what was in the barn. She tolerated, but did not approve and made her disapproval clear. I annoy her once in while by flagrantly ordering a drink when we go out for dinner. I get a glare and some verbal negativity, which I turn to humor or ignore. And she tolerates me.

We have a woman in the village who was the victim of a terrible car wreck caused by drinking and driving. She will not be found near anyone who is drinking. She does not come down to the Tree Bar. But the nice thing is that she tolerates the Tree Bar.

People with little or no tolerance for the Tree Bar represent a very small minority in the village. Alcohol, in various forms, has been an important part of human history. The reasons for that importance have not gone away.

ooo

Alcohol confers medicinal, spiritual, social, and recreational benefits. The medicinal properties of alcohol can be found in traditional as well as modern medical practice. Just the other day Bruce was saying how in his day, fifty years ago, kids who were teething had their gums rubbed with alcohol. It may have been the rubbing that brought relief, not the alcohol, but the fingers doing the massage may have come fresh from other unclean labors and the alcohol may have made the ministrations more sterile.

I can remember as a kid when alcohol was used as a cough medicine. In the Old West, alcohol was the universal anesthesia and disinfectant. Western novels and movies are replete with stories of the cowboy who took a hit and was rendered insensate by alcohol for the necessary surgery.

In many parts of the world alcoholic beverages have been a way of avoiding unhealthful water. The French have made wine drinking an art and commonly boast of wine's healthful benefits. It may be the case that alcohol and other drugs sneak into the human consciousness with their medicinal properties.

ooo

The staying power of alcohol, in human consciousness, goes beyond its medicinal properties. The spiritual properties of alcohol are manifest in human history. It is no mistake that alcoholic drinks are called spirits. Drink enough alcohol and you may find yourself visited by spirits.

The spiritual value of alcohol is apparent in the many religions that use wine as a sacrament, as the blood of the savior. Many great artists are legend for their alcohol consumption. Spirits are often associated with vision.

ooo

The social aspect of alcohol is as important as its medicinal and spiritual attributes. When people sit down and drink together, they generally do so in a relaxed environment. There is an element of trust involved when people drink together, a loosening of the tongue, a sense of relationship.

At the intimate level of socialization, Shakespeare suggested that wine could enhance desire, but could also decrease performance. The Bard touches a hard truth about alcohol and perhaps all drugs: They have benefits to a point. Individuals and societies are constantly dealing with the fine line between use and abuse.

ooo

In the Old West, as I knew it, alcohol was a prominent recreational facilitator. At the rodeo, the audience came equipped with flasks and cold beers. Music and dancing were accompanied by drinking.

It looks to me like the Old West combination of fun and alcohol is a worldwide, age-old combination. People drink because it has health benefits, because it has spiritual value, because it enhances social interaction, and because it's fun.

ooo

The Tree Bar has developed its own line between use and abuse. Drinking to the puke point is not acceptable. Drinking to the point of physical impairment is not acceptable. Drinking and verbally abusing others is not acceptable. Drunken babbling is not encouraged. Which leaves us with a slightly medicated, spiritually inclined, sociable and enjoyable participant.

An afternoon drink takes the edge off a hard day. An afternoon drink can take you away from the mechanical and electronic world and bring you down to yourself and the people who are important in your life. An afternoon drink at the Tree Bar brings you into contact with your friends and neighbors. Everybody should have one.

ooo

The standard used at the Tree Bar is different from the common USA test. The common standard used in the United States is scientific testing of the breath and the blood. The standard has become so high that almost any consumption of an alcoholic beverage is grounds for serious legal and criminal problems.

At the Tree Bar we make our judgment on the basis of behavior. We know one another and we know when one of us is going too far, is moving from use to abuse. We confiscate keys, we lecture, we demonstrate our disapproval. I know how it works because I have had my keys taken, have been lectured to, and seen disapproval in the words and expressions of my peers.

I was much younger then. But the system worked on me and I've seen it work on others. The problem with scientific testing is it fails to recognize that dosage varies from one system to another. I know people who can drink three or four times my capacity and remain fully functioning.

Instead of breathalyzers and blood tests, perhaps we should provide the constabulary with portable driving-simulation machines. We could give possible abusers the same driving test used for first-time drivers. If the potential offender cannot pass the test, he or she loses the license to drive.

The Tree Bar is an important engine of village life. The bathrooms in the park came from Tree Bar people — materials and labor. The long driveway at the side of the community hall was paved by Tree Bar community members. The patio and the pantry in the community hall are largely products of people who keep touch at the Tree Bar. The community park is maintained and groomed by well-known Tree Bar associates.

The Tree Bar is a productive focal point in community affairs. It is also a hoot. As noted earlier, Saturday night music is very entertaining. Some parents bring their kids down to play with the musicians who show up to play the Tree Bar.

For a while there, we had Elvis Presley's road horn with us. He was a washed-up sax player who still had some nice chops but was down the road as far as discipline and endurance. He had lost it somewhere along the line. But he could still play, and for an hour or two, every Saturday for a year or two, we would get to play with one of the best horn players in the country.

We have friends who have friends and the word has spread: hot music on Saturday night. Occasionally the party gets too big. Too many strangers, too many unknowns. But then, after a brief break, we get back to it. Some nights the music is marvelous, sometimes the music is simply astounding.

For many reasons the Tree Bar is a strong presence in the village. The front and sides are open to the village, and the village is open to the Tree Bar. Those of you who live in suburbia don't have Tree Bars. Nor do you have neighborhood bars as they do in Europe. Most likely you have to drive to get to a bar. In the village we keep the drinking close, and if someone gets drunk they can crawl home and take the ridicule of a community that tolerates alcohol, to a point.

The Homeless

Homelessness is one of the biggest problems facing urban units. It is also an important issue in the village. The village deals with the issue on many different levels.

I was down at the Tree Bar one afternoon when someone drove in with the news that a homeless man was walking our way, a black, crippled man with a shopping cart. To get here, he had to push his loaded cart fifteen miles from the edge of the city. We were in awe.

We can see the main road from the Tree Bar and we watched the man turn into the village. Then we saw some people from the apartments looking at the village entrance. Pretty soon, there was a small group of village people down at the county park, observing the arrival of an alien being.

It seems like the whole world is dealing with the homeless: the dispossessed, the crazies, the alienated and lonely. The homeless come in many varieties.

ooo

The most dangerous people of any social collection are those who, as Janis put it, have nothing left to lose. Our cities are full of people with nothing left to lose. San Diego, for example, like most large cities, has an incredible homeless problem.

San Diego revitalized its old downtown area only to find its efforts compromised by legions of homeless. A few years ago, I drove through the center of town and saw cardboard shacks in the doorways of renovated storefronts. Many of the storefront doorways had been used as toilets. People laid around in stupors of deprivation or over-indulgence.

The village homeless have come in many varieties. We have homegrown, migrant, subsidized, and affluent homeless. We've seen them all.

ooo

Sometimes, one of our homegrown fails in the outside world and returns for a multitude of reasons. The most personal example for me is a young man who was raised here and returned somewhat broken. I used to play basketball with him and he gave me a lot of help in my community service labors. Years after he and his family moved from the village, he returned. He was drinking hard, not working, and deep inside himself.

I'd like to say that we solved his problems, but that is not the case. We did what we could. We offered various forms of work, which he would take and, for a while, pursue. Then he would go on a binge and the work would get left behind.

At various times, he lived with various people, but his drinking was beyond control. He would end up moving from one place to another. Eventually, he started sleeping in the park. He was pretty sly, and he crashed discreetly, so that most village folk had no idea where he was staying. The ones who did know rolled with it.

He showed up every afternoon at the Tree Bar. Little by little, everyone let him know that he was giving up his life. But he persisted until his body gave out. He spent a long time in a hospital and was lucky to live. He has subsequently moved to another area where we all hope he is doing well.

The point is not that we solved his problems. Rather, we put up with him, we stuck with him, we didn't send him to town with a shopping cart. He was a known, a village product, one we all liked and knew and, yes, loved. We've dealt differently with migrant homeless people.

ooo

One homeless migrant showed up to work on some job and then just gave up any pretense of work and started mooching. No one knew this guy and no one was willing to subsidize inaction. Everyone here works; the richest and poorest people in this village work hard for their livelihood, and freeloaders are not easily tolerated. There is no such thing as spare change.

This particular example of homelessness had an origin that he spoke of with fondness. He came from such-and-such a place, and he had relatives there, and he had friends there. So we bought him a bus ticket to there, and we got him juiced up, gave him a bottle and put him on a one-way trip home.

The homeless can be a threat. Since they are generally away from home, you can never know what their history might be; maybe they are killers. In any event, they are a burden on resources.

Being of a small population, the village pays attention to the homeless. Everyone understands the potential of emotional and economic disassociation. Homelessness is as much a threat to the village as it is to the city.

ooo

A more recent and fearsome example of migrant homelessness rolled in about a year ago. He was brought in by an absentee landlord to clean up a house in sore need of repair. The homeless fellow moved in, proceeded to amaze everyone with his hard work, and was soon in great demand throughout the village.

Everyone knew he was slightly off, but his offness seemed harmless. He had a strange, filthy, neck harness around his neck, and he would engage in passionate discourse with his various selves. He became known as the one-man army; he would work until he was tired and then his other self would take over. For a while, he was a valuable village asset. But then he started saying unwelcome things to the single women of the village. As people learned of his unwelcome conversations, they stopped using his services.

Everything came to a head one day in the village market. One of the women who had been subjected to his unwelcome discourse worked in the market. Our migrant homeless man showed up at the store one morning and started an abusive conversation with the young woman. A villager walked into the store and picked up enough of the conversation to become engaged.

The villager I'm speaking of is a no-nonsense guy and will stand his ground; I'd go to the OK Corral with him. He informed the migrant that he was unwelcome and should leave.

The stranger postured for a moment or two, but eventually understood that the village man spoke for all of us having morning coffee at the front of the market. We were vigilant. I suppose you could say we were vigilantes. He left town.

I know that some of this sounds mean-spirited, but I don't think so. I think of villagers as human beings who take their responsibilities seriously and don't feel as though they need to or can take on the problems of other communities. The homeless come from somewhere — some family, some community, some state. Let them take care of their own. We have our own problems, and they are nothing but risk to us.

Our solution is very Mexican. I've spent a lot of time in Mexico, and I've always been impressed with the Mexican sense of family. I lived with one family that had a retarded child who was given daily chores, participated in family events, and was always loved. I know that things are changing in Mexico and that the large cities now have large complements of homelessness. But that homelessness is an aberration in a society that embraces familial responsibilities. My village is very much like old Mexico — we try to take care of our own.

ooo

We have also come into contact with subsidized homelessness. I mentioned earlier the incoming homeless man who had pushed his cart fifteen miles to get to us. I was at the Tree Bar, and someone dropped by to tell us that a homeless man was coming down the highway, within a few hundred yards of the village turnoff, pushing a shopping cart full of his junk.

About fifteen minutes later, I noticed that the village six-unit apartment complex was a hive of activity. Everyone was out in the parking lot looking at the turnoff to the village. Sure enough, the guy turned in and wheeled up to the library.

He spent about an hour in the library, checked out the governmental services available in the village and, finding none, he moved on down the road. He was plugged into urban subsidies.

ooo

I have experience with the urban subsidy of homelessness. As a member of my county Advisory Council, I act as a gatekeeper between the outer world and the village. The council sometimes contributes its members to committees in the urban world. For three years, because I was a longtime member of the Advisory Council, I was requested to be a part of a county committee that doles out federal dollars for the homeless.

As a member of the committee, I heard the pleas of many interest groups: religious, business, and political organizations that were trying to resolve the homeless issue. My general impression was that organized attempts to resolve the homeless issue did little other than to enable continued homelessness.

There were two men who once applied for money who did have a success rate but they never received much in the way of support. They were dressed like well-groomed homeless men, denims, flannel shirts, caps, tennis shoes, all clean. They worked at ground zero with the homeless.

They were not setting up a formal, highly funded organization. Rather, they were in the field, searching for people who had the ability to fill some community need. They helped the homeless buff up and interview for jobs that would enable them to make an income and have the hope of advancement and community participation.

The two men always looked tired, and it was obvious to me that they were working hard. But they just were not institutional enough for the general membership of the committee. There was no way they could deal with the physical and mental infirmities that lead to and sustain an incredibly large national bank of homeless.

There is an army of homeless out there pressing against our sense of civilization and decency. Their lives are not civilized or decent, and we are not civilized or decent in allowing such inhumanity. In the village, we tend to hold our own close to our chests, close to our hearts. They are ours, even though they may have gone astray, are lost and bewildered.

ooo

Despite the dangers of homegrown and migrant homeless, our biggest homeless threat comes from people who own houses but do not have homes. Everyone who moves into the village is homeless, at first, until settled in. Some people remain homeless no matter how many houses they own.

Some people buy into the village but are accustomed to the government taking care of everything. They are used to living next to people they never meet. They move here because we seem so safe, because we have created a genuine community where people take walks, talk with their neighbors, and work toward the solution of common problems. But they don't walk around the village, they don't talk with their neighbors, and they don't work for the community.

The home-owning homeless have been a real problem for the village. For example, many of them don't support the volunteer fire department, even though they have fire insurance only because our volunteers spend untold hours in training and are certified firefighters and paramedics.

Fewer and fewer people are taking care of the overall burden. One day the burden could become too much. Those serving the others will burn out, and the village will be taken over by urban governance.

If I sound a bit jaded, it's because I am. I am tired of people who love the amenities of community but feel no responsibility for that community. Many of the affluent homeless are assisting in the demise of my village and I resent them. They suck humanity out of village life.

It's not like they intend to be weenies. Some of the homeless are just so busy that they don't have time for village social interchange. I live next to a homeless house. It was built on speculation, to sell. The first buyer was a well-to-do stock/bond/money manager. He had his own radio program. Hot stuff.

My relationship with Hot Stuff began soon after he moved in. He had a Christmas party and all along his driveway he had luminaries — candles in paper bags. The day after the party, I found all the candles in the natural desert area that surrounds my house. I picked them up and threw them into his steep, grassed yard.

A few days later I was out in the front when he called me over to look at his new, jive, self-powered lawnmower. It was jammed full of grass and candle wax. "What do you think this is?" he asked.

"Why," I said, "it looks like luminario candles mixed with grass."

He was not the one who had thrown the candles into my yard but he guessed immediately that one of his kids had done the dirty deed. He looked at me; I looked at him. We moved on to other subjects.

A few months later he had his house re-stuccoed. When his guys finished up, they washed their mixers and threw their waste onto my natural desert. I loaded the waste up in my wheelbarrow and wheeled the waste into his carport.

Nothing was ever said about the stucco event. I suspect he called his guys and found out they had thrown the waste onto my property. He took it like a guy.

A few months later, Hot Stuff had a security system installed. With the slightest breeze the system would go off, and a disembodied female voice would loudly announce, over and over, "Warning Intruder, Warning Intruder." The security company had not worked out the bugs before Hot took a vacation.

The security voice box faced my bedroom. One night, after he had left for his vacation, the voice came on at two o'clock in the morning. I had been working hard and was very tired. When awakened I was enraged.

I got out of bed and, in my underwear, grabbed my five-pound sledgehammer, crawled over the low wall that separated our houses, and I beat the system off the wall onto the ground, where I proceeded to smash it into little teeny parts.

The next morning I woke up thinking it was a dream, but when I went to check it out, I found the system in tiny pieces, just like in the dream. I got a dustpan, cleaned up the mess, and threw everything away.

Several days later my neighbor came back from his vacation. He called me over to look at the hole in the wall where the security system had lived. "Look at that!" he said. "Someone stole my security system."

I said something flip to the effect that, "Yeah, there are some real low-lifes out there." He picked up something in my tone of voice, gave me a look, looked down, and then he had the hair to suggest that maybe I had done it. But then he changed the subject before I could confirm or deny the accusation.

I liked Hot Stuff, and I think he liked me. But he was a very busy man and could not be said to live here. He knew he was missing something, but his work commanded his full attention.

He never gave me any trouble over my responses to his inattention. He was a decent guy.

There are a lot of well-to-do homeless out there, decent people but people who are not quite here. We are not quite human to them, and they are not quite human to us. Sometimes we damage one another.

ooo

We have had a number of rich homeless folks who have bought a spare house here. But then, by virtue of birth, good fortune, or hard work, they see themselves as the top of the food chain, and they try to take a bite out of the village.

I don't remember his name, but a well-to-do man purchased two houses in order to collect the back lots into a possible home site. Then he tried to rezone his back lots in order to build another house.

He had so little regard for us that he bought the properties before he checked out the zoning. If the proposed zone change had been accepted, the village would have become dense, a mirror image of how people are packed together in the city.

Furthermore, we have only so much water. Each additional house means less water for existing trees and gardens. Even though everyone understood the economic advantage of suddenly having an extra house site to sell, almost everyone objected to the zone change.

The rich fellow showed up at the Advisory Council, which deals with village zone changes, and offered to build the village a tennis court if everyone would just back off their objections to his zone change. The council turned down the offer of a tennis court. The wealthy fellow did not get his way and he moved on.

ooo

From my perspective, the most destructive event to ever occur in the village involved me and a well-to-do homeless professional man who had been very successful in his career, graduated from a good university, went to a good post-graduate program, and had interned at a highly respectable institution. He is admirable in many ways.

I think he moved here to set down roots. Upon his arrival, he did not have any roots here but he joined the association that has guardianship of the village park, meeting hall, and swimming pool. He started showing up at the Tree Bar and meeting people.

But he may have tried too hard, too soon. The village fox says that we should not encourage newcomers to immediately engage in village decision- making, not until they have lived with us a while and found out what is what and who is who.

The new man jumped in early and made a few mistakes but not serious ones. For instance, he argued vehemently against startup funding for a swim program for local kids. He was worried about a program that might bring outsiders to the village. There is a village phobia, which he shares, against aliens. But that fear did not win.

The swim program turned out to be genuine blessing. Our kids learn to swim at an early age, and some of our kids have been moved to a higher level of self-esteem by virtue of their awards in regional swim contests.

Despite his occasional wrongness, our new village professional also contributed to the village talent. His occasional argument was not particularly bothersome; he seemed to take the loss of a vote as just part of life, which it is. But then he challenged a substantive village decision and became locked into what became a not-so-civil war.

The Advisory Council goes through a yearly process of debating and selecting improvements to the county park. We've gone for years without receiving additional funding. But then, suddenly, the year when a skateboard park had worked its way to our top priority, the funding materialized. We were going to get a skateboard park for our kids.

We had held a number of open meetings and discussed the skateboard park and its positive and negative aspects. We placed announcements in the post office, store, and Tree Bar — we would be voting on the matter. Most people who showed up wanted a skateboard park, and we voted for it. And then all hell broke out.

I was the chairman of the Advisory Council for ten years and have been a member for twenty years, and I have never seen a situation like this one. The man argued that somehow the system had failed. First he argued that he had not been consulted. We pointed to numerous public notices. Then he insinuated that we had somehow violated the legal processes, and he demanded a rehearing of the issue.

We agreed to a review, and the man mobilized an interesting array of allies, mostly people who had not attended to village affairs but suddenly realized they were significant.

First, he gained the support of three relatively new village mothers who thought the kids' play area should be improved before we moved to new facilities. They had a point, but they had not attended the years of discussion and so were late. As I pointed out, my wife wanted a tennis court but the people who had showed up at the meetings wanted a skateboard park.

The second argument against the skateboard park was based on an appeal to fear. The man brought our attention to the kinds of problems faced in some urban skateboard parks, and he envisioned the kind of people who might show up at our skateboard facility.

Some of the urban skateboard parks are horrible. There is not enough surveillance, and anti-social behaviors are common: graffiti, drinking, and drugs in an area designed for kids. He gained a few more supporters with appeals to our fears. Indeed, he cost me one of my most dear friends with his fear appeals.

My wife and I had a very close couple as friends and neighbors. The woman took the fear appeals seriously. She had been dealing with a lot of problems, and everyone knew she was in emotional and physical pain. In any event, she directed that pain at the proposed skateboard park.

I was the chairman of the council and so I took the heat. She never forgave me. She doesn't talk to me anymore. She flips me the bird when I drive by. I still love her. She talks with Barbara. One day she may talk with me again.

Meanwhile, the homeless professional was chugging right along. His next tack was to announce, at the Tree Bar, in front of numerous witnesses, that he was going to make my life as miserable as his. He was going to show up where I was every afternoon, at the Tree Bar, and force me to recant my evil ways. He did, but I didn't.

At first it was funny. He would show up and say things like, "Evan, when are you going to stop lying to everyone?" He would interrupt whatever we might be discussing and work me over. Being every bit the human being that he is, I responded with witticisms like, "Get a life," "Have you tried therapy?" "Maybe some religion would be good for you." We had quite a fire going.

He toyed with me, and I toyed with him. Ultimately, we were both just two players in village life. The council voted to continue with the skateboard park, and the park was built to our kids' specifications. It has been a source of great pleasure.

Several years later, none of the predicted evils has occurred. This doesn't mean that we will not have problems in the future but you don't hide in your closet because you fear outsiders. What you do is you protect what you create. In the village, that protection comes in observance, by watching over community assets.

The man was one of the first users of the park. He bought a snazzy skateboard and brought his kids down to play in the park, which is good because supervision is one of the most important parts of village life. Having adults taking walks, sitting around, yelling at everyone's kids, that's a good thing.

Even better, the homeless professional was recently seen walking with a crutch. I suspect a skateboard injury. I love it.

While we were fighting over the skateboard park, a developer sneaked in and got a significant land-use change in our area. We were not together enough to fight a significant threat to village life.

I don't hold a grudge toward the professional homeless man. I think his intent was honorable. He really had no idea what he was chipping away at when he tore at processes that have worked for all of us for a very long time. He had no idea of my friend's fragility; he had no idea that a small skateboard park was not nearly as risky as a zone change.

He is still here; he is raising his children here. At the moment, he neither adds nor subtracts from the village. He lives here but is homeless.

ooo

We have had numerous examples of how a well-to-do house owner can be homeless. Fortunately, we have also seen homeowners who do not live here but have become villagers, folks who recognize that it takes many talents to make what we have in this village, and they have contributed their talents to the village.

We have a man from New York who bought one of the bigger houses in the new section of town, on the hill, a villa. He also bought the two lots that surrounded his property. He then dropped hundreds of thousands of dollars on his home. He immediately joined the charitable association that takes care of the park, community meeting hall, pool, and Tree Bar.

Later on, when the village was pressed by an outrageous plan for 8,000 houses nearby, he supplied the buses that took us into town to fight the proposed development. The New Yorker was an alien in our Western environment, but he understood community and he contributed in meaningful ways.

He rarely visits his home in the village. In his absence, he has never had his home broken into, and village folks call him once in a while and tell him if anything looks amiss. He is welcome here.

We were all surprised. Our attitude toward New Yorkers was that they are rude, pushy, and New Yorker-Than-Thou. Our New Yorker changed our perceptions. He made a point of getting to know us, and he was willing to use his resources in defense of the village.

ooo

When you first move into a village, you are an alien. And while you may have a house, you are, at least momentarily, homeless.

One relatively new couple built a beautiful villa on the east side of the village. They and their daughter settled in with no problems. They were homeless when they first moved in, but they did not stay that way.

They appreciated what the village offered and they have contributed in many significant fashions. They built world-class horseshoe pits in the park for a popular community activity. One entrance to the park has a beautiful trellis with a climbing yellow rose, a monument to the man's mother and a marvelous addition to the village park.

Everyone who moves to the village is homeless for a moment or two, until they either get settled in or move along.

Feral Children

A feral animal is one that is not domesticated or cultivated. Traditional folk tales sometimes feature children who have been raised in the wild, who have not been domesticated or cultivated. America's cities are full of feral children.

The feral children of the city are often products of the desperately poor and/or the hopelessly addicted. As often as not, however, the feral children of the city have come from middle- and upper-class urban and suburban environments.

I don't know if it's typical, but Seattle has an incredibly large population of homeless kids. I visit the city every year and can only wonder about how it can deal with its large population of feral children. I understand that Portland, Oregon, is even worse. Those poor children.

We have had numerous feral children in the village, kids whose parents, for any number of reasons, are simply not present. Megalopolis is bulging at the seams with feral children. In the village, we have had our share.

A few years ago, there were three of them from one village family, a two-year-old, a four-year-old, and a six-year-old. I'm guessing at the ages. They were incredible little shits. They would spend whole days on their own, playing in the park, wandering through people's yards, messing with the universe.

In the village, many of us have come to the belief that once the children hit the street, they belong to all of us. And so, the feral threesome were treated as everyone's kids. Some people fed them, some admonished them against certain behaviors, some developed relationships with the parents through conversations regarding sleepovers and such.

Our recent batch of feral kids is turning out okay. They are independent, strong, and very exploratory. We love them and we're doing what we can to help them grow up.

ooo

We weren't always so smart or compassionate. Many years ago, when we faced feral children, we really were not on our toes. Most of us were amazed by their renegade behavior.

My first exposure to feral children came with a family where the father worked twelve- to sixteen-hour shifts, six and seven days a week. The mother worked a night shift. The kids had a lot of time on their own.

When we were trying to get the pool back on line, we painted the shower rooms and the pumphouse. The next day there were some pretty vulgar messages spray-painted all over the pumphouse. Someone saw the wild kid do the job. I went to the father, and he told me the kid would work with me in repainting.

I worked with the kid and had him repaint the pumphouse. I started out with a very negative attitude regarding the kid. By the time we finished the painting, I realized he was just another human being wading through an incredibly strange world.

The kid did not have a good future and died an early death. He was always too brave and reckless; he was a village James Dean. A number of village families have lost children, and some of those families have disintegrated.

Many of us who lived here at the time had the feeling we could have done better with our village son. We needed to embrace him more closely. We did better with the daughter.

The daughter had no fear. She was and is a strong and hard-working woman. In her early teens, she heard that we would be hiring a lifeguard for the pool. She went through the training, took the tests, and got the job. She was one of the first young people in the village to become a lifeguard. And she was one of the best lifeguards we've ever had.

The daughter moved on to a good career in an arduous job. She's remained in the village. I find her maddening to work with but I also find her admirable. She holds the property that the family now lives on, and she is very much at home. She takes care of everyone. And she'll take you apart if you make any negative move toward her or her family. She is kind of marvelous.

I maintain a precarious relationship with the daughter and her family. We go toe-to-toe every once in a while, and we have had some pretty stupid skirmishes. Most of the time we both realize that we both wish the best for the other. We both live here; we are village.

ooo

The village also has found that feral children can be a family tradition. Family stuff gets really interesting as you watch the apple fall from one tree, become another apple tree that in turn creates yet a third apple. We have some third-generation apples in the village who have maintained the feral theory of child-rearing.

My understanding of one family is that the feralness began in a family that had too many kids to count. Those extra kids slipped into their own lifestyle. One of those children started his own people farm and, after losing his first wife, he married a younger woman.

The father was a hard worker, gone most of the time. His children were on their own. His older son was close in age to the stepmother. Eventually he moved close in other ways. It was Shakespeare in the village.

The father, according to village rumor, with a gun in hand, chased the son down the street, much to everyone's entertainment. The village drums pumped up the volume.

Ultimately the son ended up in the house, living with his stepmother. Other children materialized. Suddenly there was a whole new crew of feral children because both the son and the stepmother put in hard hours at work and were doing their best to keep things going.

And now this progeny has produced yet another batch. The progeny from feral children has been hit and miss — some of the kids have done well, others have done poorly. I'm not really sure who belongs to whom in the house, but this new batch of feral children has been a delight to watch.

I first sighted the new batch of ferals while watering the park. There were two girls and a small boy still in diapers. They were walking the ditch line and catching toads and tadpoles. I told them that toads were becoming extinct.

They asked me what that meant, and I explained the notion of extinct. "Well, that's good," said one of the little girls. "I don't like toads anyway."

"Maybe not," I said, "but toads make tadpoles and if you keep wiping out the tadpoles, you'll run out of toads."

"I don't care," she said.

Eventually the whole village was aware of the new ferals, watching their every move and stepping in when necessary. They became village kids.

The next time I saw the new ferals they were at the bridge over the park stream. They were having a picnic, complete with lots of paper plates, cups, forks, and spoons taken from the village market.

I stopped by and chatted and, as I was leaving, asked them to make sure they buffed up the area before they left, no use leaving a mess for someone else. The next time I walked by the bridge, all the picnic gear was still spread out, in the water, over the watercress.

The next time I saw them I gave them a verbal lashing about how they had messed up their own nest. I let them know that the park was partly theirs, and they had adult responsibilities that included cleaning up your own mess. They kind of liked that, being treated like they lived here.

Our new feral children are now treated like part of the crew. And they are a delight. They have socialized with a variety of village people and are turning into well-rounded human beings — smart, decent, sensitive. Got to love them.

When I look at the number of children at loose ends in the city, I have to wonder if there is love enough to go around. In the village, we tend to be close and personal. Even if we don't exactly love one another, we try to embrace our children.

The displaced, alienated children in the cities have no one to embrace them.

ooo

Before I came to see feral kids as just another part of the stew, I viewed them in a somewhat adversarial manner. One nice afternoon, I was at the Tree Bar, alone, and a father and his feral kid drove up to the store. The kid was in the back seat. The father went into the store, and while he was inside, the kid threw a half-full soft drink can out the window.

I walked over to the rear widow and did my enraged wet chicken routine and said "Hey! You live here, you don't mess up your own nest."

"Go fuck yourself," he said, like the upstanding ten-year-old he was.

I walked back to the Tree Bar, shaking my head in wonderment. I sat and watched the kid for a while, until his attention drifted to some other kids in the park. I walked over silently, picked up the can, walked around the back side of the car, and put the can on the edge of the driver's seat.

The father came out of the store, arms full of groceries, got the door opened, and slid into the seat. There was a moment of consternation. He jumped out of the car and inspected his wet rear, looked at the can on the seat and got back into the car. The kid had no idea that his can had just wet his old man's behind.

The old man started the car. And then with a casualness that was stunning, he reached into the back seat and backhanded the kid a good one. I could see the kid protesting, and I could see his father yelling back. As they drove off, the kid was looking out the back window. I waved.

ooo

One traditional village way of dealing with kids has been work. Working children have been portrayed in the urban sense — sweatshops with long hours and little in the way of wage.

The village tradition of working children is more benign. When I think of working village children, I have in mind a village friend and mentor.

This friend had worked in hardrock mines his whole life. When he worked the Pioche mines, he would get on an elevator and go 1,600 feet into the earth and work the ore. He was a bull of a man and was reputed to have been the best driller and mucker in town.

When the Pioche mines folded, he moved to the village mine and village life. He was one of the finest men I've ever known. He put on no airs, he worked hard, he played moderately, he was decent. He had personal rules, and he lived by them.

He had three sons and a daughter. When I first moved to the village, the kids ranged from their early teens to their twenties. They lived by the house rules — no airs, everyone works. And the kids worked. They worked at home, they worked in the family business and, when they came of age, they worked jobs.

I suppose by contemporary American urban standards, the man was breaking child labor laws or, worse, abusing his children. To my way of thinking, my friend represented the old village, the vanishing village, where everyone has a vital part to play.

ooo

Mexican villages involve their children, their elderly, and their impaired. I lived with a Mexican family in the city of Guadalajara. There was a retarded son who had the jobs of sweeping and cleaning. He had to be retrained on a daily basis, and the family spent the time. It wasn't just a matter of work that needed to be done — it was matter of esteem, of having a place in the scheme of things.

My brother lives in a communal religious village in the depths of Alaska. His kids, and all the kids of his village, have chores, have a place in making things work.

Somehow the move from village to town to city to metropolis changes the position of kids, the elderly, and the impaired. They become institutionalized, and their place in the scheme of things becomes vague, remote, and less than human.

As my village has become increasingly populated by urbanites, we've seen more and more kids at loose ends. They wander around the village with nothing in particular to do. I think those kids should be given some tasks. But I'm not King and, as often as not, I can only watch the little suckers as they grow lazy, soft, and delinquent.

In looking at what I've written about the current generation of kids, I can see my rural background colors my perception. I know that many kids of urban origin do just fine. They move into structured exercise, they hit the books, they see the museums and art galleries. They are busy and they move on to become productive members of society. What many of those urban kids miss, however, is a sense of community. Their lives fit into a mass-produced culture. They maintain contact with iPods and cell phones, which they think of as private even though they are in a worldwide web.

A remarkable number of people are invading the Internet, to the point where Internet conversations are more public than private. The new mediums are forms of mass communication based on only two human senses, sight and sound — not quite the same as being in touch.

Drugs

In America, drugs tend to be divided into two classes — legally prescribed drugs and illegal, proscribed drugs. The village has seen both types. The general conclusion seems to be that there is little difference between legal and illegal drugs — they both have positive and negative effects.

The great majority of humanity has tasted the benefits of modern prescription drugs. They are directed at just about every physical and mental malady and, much of the time, they work. When a villager finds a drug that works for a given problem, other individuals with the same problem work toward the same solution. When a number of individuals have satisfactory results, the drug becomes widely used.

When a good prescribed drug is discovered, some people become mules; they head for Mexico, where they obtain their drug of choice at a reasonable price, come home and share. I suppose this is a bit corrupt, but no more corrupt than the professionals who have become mules for the legal drug companies.

For example, I recently went through a minor surgery, one that takes about a week to get past the pain. My doctor prescribed sixty pain pills, with a refill of sixty more. I took only a few of the pills before I was past the pain, past the need.

A few villagers found out that I had the excess pills, and I became deluged with offers to buy what I had left. I was offered $5-$10 for a pill that cost me eight cents (the insurance company subsidized the true cost). I could have made $1,200 on that prescription. That could have bought me a good guitar.

But I wouldn't want the responsibility of passing out my prescribed drugs. Despite their use, prescribed drugs are viewed with a great deal of skepticism in the village, a doubtful outlook based on experience. We've seen the downside of prescription drugs, drugs that solve one problem but create others, drugs that hold great promise for resolving psychological problems but result in suicidal tendencies and sometimes lead to great mayhem and sorrow.

We are particularly wary of pain pills. Several villagers have gotten hooked on a variety of pain pills. Their doctors gave them prescriptions that lasted long past the critical pain period. When their prescriptions ran out, they would buy them on the black market.

The effects of long-term use of some pain pills have become increasingly apparent to the village. The users become withdrawn from village friends, and their attitudes toward life become increasingly negative. One of the hooked villagers lost his job, his wife, and his home.

ooo

The village also has experience with proscribed drugs. Years ago, a father in the village found out that his son was addicted to heroin. The father caught his son totally incapacitated and took him to a cabin in the mountains. The father took a leave of absence from his job, and he chained his son up to a tree and every day he would feed and bathe him, talk with him, let him know that he was loved beyond all material things.

The son cried, whimpered, and beshit himself, but the father endured. Six weeks later, they came off the mountain, father and son, ready to take on the world. Nowadays it probably would be against the law to kidnap a loved one, hold him in chains, and get him past the craving. But I don't think the larger culture has a better solution.

ooo

One of the most powerful killer drugs to ever hit the village was the large-animal tranquilizer PCP, deceptively called "Angel Dust." Late one afternoon, the village was having a party in the park — lots of food, some good wines and beers, some horseshoe throwing, and a lot of good will. Some of the older boys were playing basketball with friends from town. It was a beautiful summer late afternoon.

Then one of the boys rushed from the court to tell us that one of the townies had gone crazy. And he had. About ten of the village men showed up to see what was happening. The kid was extraordinarily violent, throwing things around, attacking people, shouting obscenities.

We tried talking him down, but he was clearly not in a talking mood. He jumped one of us and it took ten of us to hold him down. I came from a world where we would jump off a horse and throw a five hundred-pound bull to the ground. And I had worked in the construction industry where physical strength was often a requirement of the job. But I have never seen power like that exhibited by the young man going crazy on our basketball court.

Within a short period, we had paramedics on the job, and they got the young man sedated. It turns out he was on PCP, the animal tranquilizer that ultimately became highly feared by all law enforcement agencies. I talked with one of our local constables who told me the story of a man on PCP who took numerous hits from high-powered guns and kept on coming.

I understand that PCP has become relatively rare. I think the rarity is based on both official and community standards. Everyone decided that PCP should not be used by human beings. We call these kinds of drugs "poison."

ooo

In the village, drugs are viewed in a number of different ways. We all know there are killer drugs and we don't want them anywhere around. There are also drugs that are generally tolerated.

Through trial and error, the village has come to accept some drugs while rejecting others. Prescribed and proscribed drugs are viewed equally. Indeed, illegal drugs are as easy to obtain as the legal ones. A village father of a teenage son once noted that it was easier for his son to get heroin than beer.

After decades of the war on drugs, it looks to me as though most people could care less about marijuana. Few are buying the "gateway drug" theory regarding marijuana. There are now generations of doing-well people who have found marijuana to be a good alternative to prescribed relaxants. It also seems like a lot of people find marijuana entertaining.

As in the larger culture, marijuana is widely accepted in the village. It is understood that the drug is illegal. Aside from that, the general feeling is that marijuana has enough positive effects to be a home remedy. It probably should be an over-the-counter drug.

There are some people in the village who use grass to keep from going postal. There are people who are extremely nervous, for whatever reason, who use marijuana to relax. There is an underground that supplies marijuana to cancer patients.

There are also people who use grass as a recreational drug, one that is much more gentle than the legal drug of alcohol. These people tend to stay put, not get into fights, and they enjoy food. The consensus is that grass is a happy drug.

ooo

The village maintains a steady zero-tolerance policy regarding kids and drugs. We've had some people who have thought that getting their kids high was okay. Most of us ride with Aldous Huxley, who argued that one of the biggest effects of drugs is to rob the will.

It's one thing for a fully developed adult to become momentarily will-less. His or her path has been chosen, his or her talents have already been established. But with kids we've seen that early drug use can lead to a life of vacuity. We prefer to have our kids on their toes and moving.

We've also had examples of adults who are sloppy with their drugs, who do not keep them out of the hands of children. For instance, we had a man in the village who was heavily involved in some of the more powerful speeds and downers. One day, his kid got into the drugs and shared with other kids in the village. For about two days, we had a bunch of really loony kids on our hands.

A group of us traced the origins of the problem, met the man in his front yard, and suggested he should move, underlined by the threat of legal action. He left. He may have gone back to where he came from. He may be in your neighborhood now. If you love your kids, better pay attention.

In more anonymous environments, big cities, for example, drugs tend to exist beyond any community standard. In the village, community standards have pretty well dictated what drugs are acceptable. I like those standards. They are real. They work. There is some trial and error that can lead to problems, but we do not have the problem generated by the lack of community found in urban environments.

ooo

Drugs may have their own delimiting character. One night in Amsterdam, I saw a group of young people shooting up heroin. I know what it was because I asked them, and they were candid. Later I was in a bar where a businessman and I got to talking. He asked me what I thought about Amsterdam, and I told him I liked it, I liked its humanness, and I liked its openness. I also noted that I was disturbed by the hard drug use I had seen on the street.

His response was that if you have a destructive trait, you will work that out, one way or another. Perhaps, he said, you will go crazy and shoot vast numbers of people like you do in America. Maybe you will commit suicide. That's where hard drugs come in. In choosing drugs as your way to go out, you are also diminishing the gene bank that may harbor the desire to self-destruct.

While clever, I'm not sure if my Amsterdam acquaintance is correct in his assessment. One of my best friends has a brother who recently died at age forty-eight after many years of hard drug use. He had several children and grandchildren. And when you look at inner-city America, you see an abundance of killer-drug parents with kids who are addicted before they are born.

ooo

The village perspective on drugs may not be the best, but it works most of the time. We still have a problem with kids and grass. Not everyone views grass as a problem, yet most of the village would agree that kids and grass are not a good combination. But the kids are getting their stuff from town, and we have a hard time controlling that flow.

We can and do identify the older teens involved and let them know that as the oldest of their peer group, they will be held responsible if any of the kids are caught smoking grass. We do the same with booze: let the older kids and young adults know that they are responsible for any harm that comes from giving drugs to kids.

We know some of the kids party in the park at night. They drink some beer, get a little drunk, and throw up all over themselves and their friends. Some people don't see what's going on, but those who do tend to tolerate a little drinking. It's almost a ritual of growing up, and better they find out the downside of drinking here than in a car, driving down the road in the dark of night.

ooo

The anti-drug interest groups are absolutely right in their belief that drugs can destroy lives. They are also absolutely wrong in their approach to controlling drugs.

The prescribed/proscribed approach has led to some amazing hypocrisies. Legal drug companies crank out an abundance of drugs that outnumber the medical need. Those drugs find their way to a black market. Some of the illegal drugs are commonly known to be benign.

The village solutions to drugs has been basic. We place as much oversight on legal prescriptions as we place on illegal drugs and have developed community standards regarding illegal drugs. The same can't be said for megalopolis.

Public Urination

I've seen people urinating on the streets of New York, Madrid, Paris, Seattle, Chicago, and Mexico City. The best public urination I've seen occurred one night as I was sitting in a nice restaurant in Andorra, Spain, at the dead end of a road from the ski lift. The large window facing the lift was made of one-way glass. The street was dimly lit.

Three men came staggering down the street. They were obviously a bit drunk and quite comradely. They had their arms around one another's shoulders and were laughing and having a good time.

They came to the road's end and were deciding which way to turn when they made the collective decision to have a little relief at the wall of the tall building in front of them. They walked right up to the window thinking it was a solid black wall, and, with backs straight, hands down holding their equipment, staring straight ahead (as men do), with expressions of great satisfaction, they proceeded to take a long leak.

Meanwhile, in the restaurant everyone was enjoying the show. The kids made their way to the window and, in French, Spanish, German, and English, made a variety of hilarious observations regarding the members of the three men. The women in the audience also enjoyed the show. We men watched with manly recognition and some mirth.

What I found of most interest in the Andorra experience was the non-Puritan response to public urination. Civilized people tend to avoid public urination, but here I was at a hub of European civilization and the auditors were not clamoring for the death penalty.

ooo

My American village is a bit provincial when it comes to public urination. One of the biggest battles in village history started with a case of it. It was a Saturday night, the Tree Bar was cooking, the music was going strong, the drinking was steady. One of the miners went into the park to take a leak behind a bush.

Unfortunately, a village mother was standing at the edge of the park and could see the backside of the miner and knew what he was doing. All hell broke out.

At the time, the observant mother was stressed out by a number of personal problems in her life. The backside-sighting was just one too many irritations. She came unglued and, the next day, the whole world became aware that some public urination had been happening in the village.

There were ominous notes pinned on the village bulletin boards. Within a few days, the public urination turned into blatant public exposure. Soon there was a call for a general meeting.

The community hall was packed; we had police enforcement just in case those public urinators put up a fight. We had strangers in dark suits who stood around the edge of the crowd. It was quite a show.

The mother started the meeting with heavy pathos. What a sad day when her children could look out the window and see some guy wagging his member in full view. How uncivilized, how crude, how perverse! Shudder.

After thirty minutes of some serious breast-beating rhetoric the miner confessed and politely apologized if he had upset anyone. He also went on to point out that it was dark, his dick was in the bush, and whoever saw him must have been at least three hundred feet away. He also allowed as how the event was blown way out of proportion.

Others spoke in his defense, and the meeting finally ended with the resolution to build a bathroom in the park. The bathroom, like the Tree Bar, came into being by virtue of critical inquiry.

In a village you don't just overlook someone's serious objections. Even if the objections seem frivolous, the people making them are real enough, and they, too, are part of the village.

I suspect that one of the characteristics of village life is that criticism, while not particularly welcome, is tolerated. If the criticism has merit, enough people roll and changes are made. And life goes on. I wrote a song about it:

Here's a story of a man we all know
a regular cowboy, a regular fellow
He'd come to the park on weekends, tell stories and lie
drink with his friends until the evening would die
Suddenly his life changed
he was no longer a wrangler
suddenly he was
the midnight dangler.

We were having a good time
he was drinking with me
and we both went out looking for a tree
He went one way, and I went the other
that's when it happened, please call his mother.
Suddenly his life changed
he was no longer a wrangler
suddenly he was
the midnight dangler.

How was he to know that far away at the edge
there was a lurking mother peering through the hedge
It was dark and dingy and she was far away
but she knew she was seeing foul play
Suddenly his life changed
he was no longer a wrangler
suddenly he was
the midnight dangler.

She could only see his backside
but she knew what he had in his hand,
he was standing there drawing little fishies in the sand
She hated that, public urination
when she got through with him
he'd feel her righteous indignation
Suddenly his life changed
he was no longer a wrangler
suddenly he was
the midnight dangler.

The next day at the PO there was lots of mouth BO
rumors and innuendoes, do you intiendo?
A million words later she finally ran out of steam
Now every Saturday night,
she waits at the edge of the hedge
do you know what I mean?

Suddenly his life changed
he was no longer a wrangler
suddenly he was
the midnight dangler.

ooo

No one wants to see public urination — it just doesn't seem right. It's not pretty. It's also a health hazard, and it smells. Both city and village folks find themselves having to deal with the issue. I think the issue is somewhat symbolic — are we animals?

The village has not yet found the solution. We had our big public urination event and built a restroom in the park. But about a year ago, I noticed that someone was relieving himself on an outside wall of the restroom, on a concrete slab that stains quite nicely with human urine.

I think I know the teenager who is doing the pissing. He has recently taken to pissing in the Tree Bar. Ugh, good gork!

I don't go to the parents because I know that they, too, are at a loss as to how to handle their offspring. I could talk to the kid, but he would deny it, as he's denied other offenses against his neighbors.

This is not nice, but I've also thought a good beating might help the kid. He's pissing on us, a very physical act, and laughing at our attempts to cope with his out-of-hand actions. I've seen this before, and remain helpless.

Years ago, there was teenager who engaged in a number of incredibly anti-social behaviors, including destructive physical acts. Everyone tried to talk the kid down. The father did his best but the kid was hell-bound. He got away with a lot of gross behavior in the village. But one night, when he reached driving age, he tried his hard ways downtown. And he got the shit beat out of him.

And so the village pisser is getting away with it, for now. What the dumb guy doesn't understand is that there really is karma. He'll wag his weenie in the wrong place one day, at the wrong time, and in front of the wrong people, and he will be labeled as a deviant. This is what I and others have told the young man.

The village solution to public urination has taken two approaches. First, we've provided a facility that takes care of what is sometimes an immediate need. Second, we dish out a good deal of generally expressed ridicule regarding the few covert pissers who show up once in a while. Other than an occasional deviant, the issue of public urination is not significant.

In the city, public urination is a significant problem because of the large number of homeless people. They do not have personal facilities, and commercial operations are not keen on having noncustomers using their resources — their space, their water, their paper products, their cleaning service. And so the burden falls on public facilities not funded by those who use them.

If urban areas were viewed as a number of small communities (villages), the far-from-home homeless would be shuffled out of the community and delivered back to their places of origin. This may not be the best of solutions, but I suspect that public urination will remain an ongoing urban issue as long as homelessness is treated as an institutional rather than a personal problem.

Relationship With Nature

One traditional characteristic of the village is that it never loses sight of nature. My village has a number of domesticated and wild life forms.

In terms of flora, villagers have gardens and trees by virtue of hard work and perseverance — the desert is a harsh mistress. We are also blessed in that our village has native trees. Our flora make an otherwise inhospitable environment livable and pleasant. Sometimes we even indulge in the luxury of growing giant pumpkins.

For those of us who have roots in the desert, the village is particularly symbolic — it is our oasis. I can remember as a kid riding for many hours in order to reach a spring with a patch of green. That green represented life to me and to all the native plants and animals that relied on the oasis for water, shade, and habitat.

I particularly appreciate trees. As a kid, I was a good climber of trees, and I carried the trait into adulthood. When Barbara and I first moved to Las Vegas, my tree-climbing ability came into good use. We lived in a house that had at one time been on the outskirts of town and was becoming increasingly urban, with sidewalks and street lamps.

We had a seventy-foot cottonwood tree that was fifty feet from the house. One day I noticed that the tile in the bathroom was lifting up. I starting lifting tiles and found a fine web of roots originating from the sewer line — the tree had pierced the line and found its way into the house. It was incredible.

The tree punctuated our lives in many ways. During a high wind, one of the big limbs dropped and we were lucky to not lose part of our roof. The tree also formed a canopy over the street. I came to the conclusion that the tree needed to be pared back. That cottonwood was seventy feet tall and its limbs spanned half the road.

I roped my way up, straddled the high limbs, and began the grooming. It took me several days to trim it back to a point just short of death. All my neighbors were appalled. They said that I had killed the tree, that I had removed a neighborhood icon. And so forth.

The tree came forth the next spring, and every two or three years I would cut the new growth back by two-thirds. In short, I bonsaied a big tree, and it worked. I went back fifteen years later and the tree was still there, not a liability overhanging the public street. All the other large trees along the street had been removed.

When we moved to the village, our home had several large elms, most of which were encroaching over my roof. As I noted earlier, my tree talent came to good use when we moved to the village. During one particularly aggressive year, I trimmed or removed forty ungroomed and risky trees.

For a short time, I also made money with my tree craft. I made a very good wage trimming and grooming the trees at one of the oldest ranches in the canyon. I have also, as part of my community service, taken care of the more than one hundred trees in the community park. I am also a wood sculptor and appreciate the beauty and grain of all our trees.

I bother with this somewhat long recital of my tree-hugging past in order to bring you up to date on a village issue that reflects just how far our controlling urban government has become removed from nature.

ooo

I recently went to get the mail and noticed that a large number of our trees had been marked with pink ribbons. It turned out they had been marked for death.

The execution order stemmed from an event that started on Sunday night, January 27, 2008, with eighty-mile-per-hour winds. A tree on the county easement blew over and flattened a neighbor's fence. He called the county, which first disputed that the tree was its responsibility. He pushed and proved his point.

In early February, the county came out and removed the tree. And while it was at it, it ribboned our roadway trees for death. I talked with the road crew and found out that the county logic was that the trees were a liability and, rather than maintain them, they would simply remove them. Simple thinking indeed.

Needless to say, lots of people were irked for a number of good reasons. First, the tree that fell, fell because the county, several years ago, had dug a trench along the road and severed all the roots on one side of the tree. It should have, at the time, removed the tree. The county created a crisis, and now it was using the fallen tree as a pretext for eliminating all the trees rather than nurturing and caring for them.

Second, the county method of accounting was faulty. The county planned to farm out the tree removal at a cost of about $1,000 per tree. Some of the marked trees are perfectly healthy and in good shape. One person with a chain saw could prune and maintain such trees for about $100 per tree per year. A good pruning will last for two to five years, depending on the tree. In other words, many of those trees marked for death could be good for another thirty to forty years for the price the county was willing to pay for their destruction.

Furthermore, if we went to buy some of the trees marked for destruction, we would find the value to be somewhere around $20,000 to $50,000.

Also, there was this: The county process in this matter was disturbing. The people who live here had not been consulted on the matter of our public easements. We argued that we pay our taxes and would like some say in how our village looks. Let's do the reasonable thing, let's walk through the village with our public service representatives and negotiate what needs to go and what needs to stay. That's what we said.

We were assured that the county would hold a meeting in the village to discuss our trees. It was hoped that we could negotiate some understanding between our urban government and the villagers.

ooo

On Monday, February 12, 2008, before a meeting regarding the trees, a public works crew rolled in with chain saws, a commercial chipper, and a dump truck. Before anyone knew what was happening, the crew had removed two twenty- to thirty-year-old mesquite trees.

I e-mailed our county liaison and informed him that the county was knocking out our trees before our agreed-upon meeting. He contacted a representative of public works. He was told that the crew was only going after shrubs blocking vision at intersections. Apparently his crew did not know that the mesquite can be trained as a bush or a tree. The *New Western Garden Book* notes that the mesquite is one of the "trees that helps make outdoor living more comfortable in the desert."

Several people called our county commissioner, and our liaison assured us that no more trees would be cut down until the meeting. We thought the situation was stable.

But then, on February 13, 2008, Public Works snaked in and knocked off two more mesquite trees and were working on the oldest fig tree in the village. Unbelievable.

The fig tree is an important icon in the village. Figs are very hard to grow here, but seventy or eighty years ago, some settler planted one, just to see. The tree has had a hard life. Once in a while, we have an extremely cold winter and the poor tree dies back — only to emerge again, like a Phoenix, and supply summer fruit to birds and village folk alike.

I received a phone call from a very irate villager and when I arrived on the murder scene there were already fifteen or twenty people who had shown up to register their disgust. I did my enraged wet chicken routine, and someone called a television station. With the village leaning on them, the crew left. Now, after more phone calls and e-mails, we are again set for a cease-fire until our meeting.

Our urban masters are incredibly out of touch with their rural territory. They don't know how precious a tree is in the desert. And they are strapped with an incredibly complex communication system — to move an issue from ground zero to a commissioner can take a week as the message filters through one level of government after another.

ooo

The mesquite is my favorite of all desert flora. It is a beautiful, tough, and fruitful tree. It will grow thirty to forty feet tall and can also develop multiple trunks and spread out over a vast area. It has long, fern-like dark green leaves and a pronounced yellow seed pod, like a bean pod.

One estimate is that twenty-five percent of the planet has one or another variety of mesquite tree. They grow in low-elevation desert valleys and they can survive up to levels of 5,500 feet. They are incredibly drought resistant and send out a sponge-like mass of roots that strangle other competing flora. According to some reports, mesquites will also send down tap roots as far as 150 feet.

Adding to their fetching nature is the fact that mesquites are fruitful. Mesquite beans are nutritious and versatile. Numerous food products can be made with mesquite beans. Soaked and strained, the beans make a tasty tea. Ground and fermented, they make a delicious wine. Used as a spice, mesquite bean flour can be used as a topping on ice cream, yogurt, cookies, and so forth. The flour can be used with any other flour as a valuable nutrient and flavoring. Breads, cakes, cookies, and all baked goods are enhanced with the use of mesquite flour.

Native Americans used every part of the mesquite tree. The leaves were used as a therapeutic tea. Honey from mesquite flowers was prized. The bark was made into a fiber and used in weaving and baskets. The wood was burned. The seed pods were ground into incredibly nutritious flour and were an important part of the diet. Coyotes, deer, burros, sheep, goats, cattle, and horses all eat the bounty provided by the mesquite.

The first white settlers were not quite so savvy. They were aware that the Indians used the tree in numerous ways, but the settlers only used the tree for firewood, tool handles, and furniture. They lacked the technology necessary to crack the fibrous, hard, and oily seed pod. They had mechanized stone grinders used for wheat, corn, and other hard grains, but such grinders clog up with mesquite oils and fibers.

Modern mega-agriculture has tended to view the mesquite as a pest. It takes over pasture areas, it crowds out domesticated fruit trees and bushes. Western cities have destroyed thousands of acres of mesquite in the press to pave paradise. The mass destruction of mesquite has significantly diminished fauna fodder. The destruction has also had negative human consequences.

The mesquite bean is a superb human food, high in protein, carbohydrates, fiber, and sugar while low in fat and cholesterol. The bean is roughly twenty percent fructose sugar and thirty-five percent protein. The fructose sugar can be absorbed without the use of insulin and, because of the fiber content, mesquite flour is absorbed slowly. Indian populations that fed on mesquite beans had a low rate of diabetes; now some of those populations, eating contemporary foods, are plagued by a high rate of diabetes. Go figure.

There is great irony in imagining the early Southwest settlers starving while surrounded by mesquite manna. There is equal irony in the contemporary destruction of a plant that is drought resistant and a sustainable agricultural crop in otherwise inhospitable environments.

As the American Southwest continues into what appears to be an abiding drought, the mesquite is an increasingly important tree. The urban masters of rural agriculture have yet to understand the situation. Farming in the Southwest is becoming increasingly difficult and we should be moving into transitional agriculture. We should be inter-planting mesquite trees in fruit groves. We should be replacing vine fruits with an indigenous, drought-resistant, fruiting plant such as the prickly pear. If only they would make me king.

Mesquite trees are spiny and hard to hug, but as you can tell, I've come to embrace them. That's why, when an urban power starts mowing down local mesquite trees, I start jumping up and down, along with my friends and neighbors.

ooo

The county, to its credit, changed its stand on trees in the public easement. Our roadside trees are now trimmed and provide shade and firewood. Best of all, our burros, coyotes, and other fauna, including the human variety, have bonded with mesquite trees. We have established a relationship with our flora. Step back, we have the wisdom of trees.

ooo

Fauna has been as important to the village as flora. When I first moved to the village there was an active 4-H organization and people raised hogs, cattle, goats, sheep, rabbits, chickens, and turkeys. There was a large, shared corral area a quarter-mile from the village. Much of the village meat came from the village corral.

As more urbanites moved into the village, animal husbandry decreased. Then the federal government closed down the corral.

The corral was on federal land and had been so from the beginning of remembered time. The feds gave the village a choice. If we would develop a commercial arena for mass entertainment, then we would be allowed to continue raising farm animals. We decided that we did not want a commercial enterprise of that scale next to the village, and we lost a big chunk of our animal husbandry.

Even with the loss of our corral area we still had two strong rural elements: dogs and wildlife. Many years ago, the dogs of the village, like the people, were engaged in a physical struggle to survive. Like the men, the dogs took no shit, and dogfights were common.

As the village became more civilized, the nature of our dogs changed. We started getting "fluffies," those cute little designer doggies engineered for cuddling. Needless to say, the people with the fluffies did not like the big killers that wandered the village. Little by little, the killers disappeared.

But dogs, being a versatile lot, have survived as village assets. I can walk my dog through the village on a soft summer night and get all the dogs in the village barking in sequence as I move from one street to another. It's quite a symphony, and an early warning system.

Most people now keep their dogs behind fences, and their primary function is early warning. I can sit on my porch and know someone is moving through the village by listening to the various dogs doing their jobs. I have their voices down and can just about tell you where the peace is being disturbed.

The wolves are particularly neat. We have a pair of semi-domesticated wolves in the village. They can hear a siren long minutes before a human. They have a soulful sound and dominate the howls that sometimes resound throughout the village.

The most interesting dogs in the village have been those that moved from a particular home to the village at large. These are clever dogs, and the suspicion is that they may be a superior species.

Abby, for example. There is a picture of Abby in the village market. She is lying on the floor at the center of the store, where she used to take her afternoon nap. The picture makes it clear that this dog has friends in high places.

Abby had a base of operations, a home where she was loved, but she was a cruiser. Her favorite cruise spot was the village market, where she could share treats with her human equals and meet everyone in the village. Touroids thought she was just adorable and would buy expensive jerky for her gastronomic pleasure.

I had one of those village dogs, Goldie. She was a sleek one hundred-pound Labrador. When we lived at the center of the village, Goldie was a favorite of the village mothers. Kids could climb all over Goldie and she loved it. Mothers would let Goldie into their homes as a kind of baby-sitter. And of course, those mothers would feed her treats.

Our current village dog is Buster. He was picked up in town, a bag of bones and insecurities. He now weighs somewhere around forty pounds and is fairly healthy. The villager who saved Buster from the city streets took care of him, fed him, and made sure he had his shots.

Unfortunately, the master was a very busy man and Buster was often on his own. Being slightly smarter than his master, Buster escaped at will. Eventually he found various homesteads that were welcoming and rewarding. He soon became the village dog. It's not like Buster is some beauty queen. He has some strange skin condition and has lost most of his hair from the neck back. He is gray and his fluffy neck hair gives way to what looks like a pigskin back. One of our local vets is working on the hair problem.

Despite his disreputable look, Buster is very charismatic. He approaches people with a deferential attitude and is totally non-threatening. He'll approach people sitting at the front of the store, and if the people are engaged with one another, Buster will pick a likely looking victim and sidle up next to him or her. Then, with exquisite timing, he will raise one paw and gently touch his victim's leg. And when the victim looks down, Buster gives him the pleading look, the "I'm homeless and starving" look. The mark generally goes into the store and comes out with some goodies. Some of the miners buy bags of dog biscuits that are kept at the store and passed out at the beginning and ends of work shifts.

Buster now generally spends his nights at one home or another and then visits the store, post office, and bike shop, where he allows his subjects to give him treats. And then he spends the day wandering around from house to house, with occasional re-visits to the shops where he works the touroids.

This last winter was a cold one and Buster needed a coat. A collection jar was allowed in the store, and Buster ended up getting five new coats. I think he liked the coats, and he did look pretty flashy.

Buster recently had a runny eye problem. Sadly, it turns out that he had a malignant growth on one eyelid. Buster had to lose an eye. A local vet agreed to do the surgery with no promise of payment. A collection jar at the store did well and Buster got his needed surgery. Some people wanted to see Buster with a glass eye, while others thought an eyepatch would be cool.

I suppose it's stupid to get so attached to an animal. But since we like to think we are the masters here, we need to pay attention to our responsibilities.

ooo

Watching the village dogs is instructive. My wife and I once had a really nasty dog, Tres. Our daughter brought Tres home and we suffered the consequences. The dog hated all other animals and loved nothing better than to attack. In retrospect, I think she was a fear-biter, she feared just about everything and went on the attack before she could be attacked. There are people who are like that, too.

Anyway, Tres was not stupid and she knew that the best time to train a dog was when it was young and small. She showed us how that early training worked with Sam, a young Labrador of world-record size. He was also just as cute as all get out, and Tres hated him at first sight, knew he needed to be put in his place.

One hot summer day, down at the Tree Bar, Tres was sitting under one of the tables while I was having a cold beer. Tres weighed about forty-five solid, muscled pounds. The pup, Sam, weighed about twenty pounds.

Sam walked by the table and Tres reached out, grabbed his lower lip and bit down slowly, but surely, until she drew blood. When Sam was on his knees and whining pathetically, she let him go and he ran off into the park.

From that time on, for the next year or so, if Sam saw Tres he would make a big circle around her. He wanted nothing to do with her. And she liked it that way. She was the boss. She had established her dominance.

For a while, I thought Tres might have had a winning combination, one that just might relate to human behavior. But a year or so later, I had to revise my estimate of the lesson.

At several years of age, Sam became homeless — his owner could no longer keep him. We took him in. Tres was not happy with that move. She would lay in the hallway, blocking the way to the food bowl. She would lay in the hall that blocked the bedroom where we slept. She tormented Sam at every chance. By this time, Sam outweighed Tres by sixty pounds and could have put her neck in his mouth, but he had been conditioned to fear her.

I was on the phone, in the house, when that fear was overcome. I heard screaming on the front porch and ran out to find

Tres shivering and shaking. Sam was off to the side, looking guilty, head hanging down, avoiding eye contact, tail between his legs.

I examined Tres and found a circle of saliva around her neck. She wasn't bleeding, but she was in shock. When I opened the door to go back into the house, she darted in, ran to her bed in a back room, and stayed there for a day or two.

When Tres emerged, she was a different animal. She no longer tormented Sam. The nice thing is that he was decent enough not to rub it in. He never messed with her, and he was never messed with by her, from that time on. Aren't those animals something?

ooo

The wild animals, like the domesticated animals around the village, are fun to observe. When I first moved to the village, I often saw deer in the community park. Once in a while I would see a mountain sheep behind my house. Wild horses were common, as were coyotes, roadrunners, rattlesnakes, and burros.

As the city has approached, the wildlife has receded. The sheep, horses, and cougars are gone. I tend to think of the village as a borderland, a place that resides between the wild and the civilized, between the rural and the urban, between nature and man. And so I've viewed the demise of our wildlife as a diminishment of village life.

But all is not lost. We still have enough wildlife to keep us in touch with Mother Nature. Last year a pair of coyotes started making early-morning and late-evening visits to my neighbor's apple tree. It was late fall and the apples were the easiest and best fodder.

A few weeks ago, a coyote was run over in the canyon. I suspect it was the male of the pair working my neighbor's apple tree because now the female is foraging on her own.

Burros have been commonplace in the village. They were the prospectors' truck. Burros are drought-resistant, hard-working beasts. They are also ornery and independent.

Once, as a teenager, I was in the outback and did not hobble my horses right. The next morning I found myself afoot, many miles from home. I was near a spring and was lucky enough to find and rope a wild burro. I haltered the burro, jumped on, and went for the most aggravating ride of my life. At first the burro ran, but then came to a sudden stop. I stayed on, which is generally better than falling off. Then I tried to get the burro to move. I kicked the burro in the ribs and it just stood there. At my most vigorous kick, the burro took advantage of my precarious hold and started some evasive action. We ran through a mesquite tree that left me bloodied and hurting.

Then we stopped again. Finally, its ribs sore from steady booting, the burro moved, and we made our way back to the ranch, slowly, with many interesting side trips. That damned animal walked me right into a saguaro — a tall cactus with a central trunk full of two- and three-inch spikes.

I eventually got home, but I think the burro won. We let the burro go and I'll bet she never allowed another human being within twenty feet — I know how she feels.

While the wild horses that used to frequent the village have disappeared, the burros have maintained a steady presence. The Bureau of Land Management, which mismanages wild horses and burros, periodically rounds up the burros and sells the best ones. The remaining animals are let loose in a different range.

Some of the burros are very savvy. Old Lop Ears, for example, managed to hang around here for somewhere around fifteen years. He was a vigorous youth and sired many children. Sometimes his herd would contain eight to ten females. He was a busy burro.

Old Lop Ears was a powerful figure in the burro community. One of his main jobs was keeping all the young male burros from sneaking in and helping themselves to the many available females.

Lop Ears was evasive. He confounded the best minds of the Bureau of Land Management, which some say was no great feat. The BLM does an occasional roundup of the burros. One night, we would have burros in our yards, eating our rosebushes, and then the next night there would be no burros in the valley, except Old Lop Ears and a few of his favorite burritas. He was sneaky.

He was captured once and penned up with all the other losers. The village drums spread the word. The BLM was beleaguered with outraged phone calls — how dare they remove such an important canyon icon? To make a long story short, Old Lop Ear ended up back on the street. Which is what killed him.

The state raised the speed limit on the road through the canyon to facilitate traffic around the growing urban center. In the first year of increased speed, the road took the lives of twenty-two burros, two wild horses, numerous coyotes, owls, and roadrunners, and two humans. One of the burros was Old Lop Ears. He took the hit right at the entry to the village. The price of progress.

ooo

Wild birds have been an enduring pleasure for village folks. In particular, roadrunners are a never-ending hoot. The battles between roadrunners and coyotes have been the stuff of many cartoons.

Roadrunners are members of the cuckoo family, which has a humorous ring, but in reality the bird is a vicious, mean raptor, a tyrannosaurus rex in miniature. If roadrunners were larger, we humans would be running for our lives.

We have two roadrunners that work our homestead and have cleaned out the lizard and snake population. We were both surprised and chagrined when we found that the roadrunners also eat other birds and ground squirrels. They particularly delight in sparrow alfresco.

Every once in a while, we'll hear a scream and see a road-runner heading off into the sunset with a sparrow in it mouth. The sparrows have gotten real cautious but the roadrunners are fantastic hunters. Every day they seem to make their quota. When pickings get slim, the roadrunners move along, only to return the following year.

Each day is different for the roadrunners. Sometimes a road-runner will come in over the roof and drop down on the sparrows in the front yard. Sometimes the roadrunner will arrive in the evening, sometimes in the morning.

One morning, while working in my study, I saw a roadrunner hunkered down in the pyracantha hedge. An hour later I took a break from my work and looked out the window; the road-runner was still there. About a half hour later, I heard sparrows and looked out the window to see a herd of them, out of easy reach in another part of the hedge, chittering and chatting and letting the roadrunner know that they were on to him. I think he went without breakfast that day.

ooo

We have a lot of birds in the village, sparrows, mountain finch, juncos, hummingbirds, quail, dove, hawks, eagles, and so forth. And we have Elvis.

We think Elvis blew in on the end of a tropical storm from some Latin American jungle. Elvis is a magpie jay. He is not listed in *Peterson's Field Guide to Western Birds*. He is an out-of-towner.

Elvis is a flashy bird. He has a tail that is longer than his body. His colors seem to change throughout the year. Mostly, he is blue with some white, and he weighs in around ten pounds.

Elvis settled into village life and, much to everyone's surprise, he made it through a winter. Word spread and pretty soon members of the Audubon Society were showing up in flocks with binoculars and bird books. Elvis had his fifteen minutes of fame.

Elvis has survived despite the harsh environment, probably because he seems to eat just about anything. He's been seen with a mouse, with dog food, with unidentifiable substances. He looks well-fed.

He has now been with us for about five years. One day, a village woman asked a world-known ornithologist what would happen if poor Elvis never found a mate. He told her that the bird probably would live a long, satisfying life. And he has. There is some irony in the fact that Elvis has outlived the ornithologist.

The hawks take a look at his size and his strong nut-crunching beak, and they leave him alone. The ravens hound him, but it looks like good sport, and he seems to have handled them. In short, he likes village life.

ooo

Many years ago rattlesnakes were common visitors to the village. When we first moved here, George, the miner whose home we bought, had left behind a quart jar full of rattles from snakes killed at the mine and on the road. I assumed he had killed the snakes at the mine, but we had no sooner moved in when we found a rattlesnake on our back porch. I killed the snake.

A few years ago, Ruby, a marvelous greyhound mix, started raising hell on the front porch. I had raised a good garden that year, and the ground squirrels had developed a taste for tomatoes. Snakes like ground squirrels. A Panamint rattlesnake found its way to the garden, had a ground squirrel for lunch. and then decided to sun itself on the front porch. Ruby took exception to that.

Panamints are not as deadly as the Mojave rattler but their bite is not to be taken lightly. They are not a particularly aggressive snake and, unlike a sidewinder, they will not chase you if you happen to wander too close. They rattle a lot and tend to be very territorial — they expect you to go away.

But the Panamint on the front porch wasn't about to give up its place in the sun. I had the neighbors over for a look and pretty soon we had a good-sized crowd of people and dogs surrounding the snake.

Finally, I rounded up a container and got the snake boxed. I drove the Panamint ten miles from the village and released it.

The release was a sea change for me. In my youth, on the ranch, we killed every rattlesnake we found — they were dangerous for our stock and they were dangerous to us. Our attitude was fairly common in the Southwest.

At the time we found the Panamint on the porch, wildlife had become increasingly scarce. From the beginning of time, snakes have been a part of the garden, representative of the choice human beings face. It has been years since a rattlesnake has been seen in the village; they seem to have reached the vanishing point.

My attitude has changed from one of aggression to one of pity. Urban encroachment and thousands of tourists have thinned the wildlife. Part of my apprehension regarding the vanishing village is the vanishing wildlife.

ooo

Recently one of the semi-urbanized village kids was eating some potato chips and happened to read the label. "Wow," he said, "these things are made from potatoes." That's both funny and sad. Urban life typically does not include contact, understanding or appreciation of nature. As villages turn into towns and towns turn into cites and cities turn into megalopolis, we lose sight of nature. We ruthlessly exploit nature more and more as we gouge out minerals, nutrients, water, and life from increasingly large segments of the earth. We have become a plague.

Junk

Traditionally, in small village settings, human waste is not a significant problem. But when the human herd obtains a certain size, village solutions no longer work.

Junk has been one of the more common and valuable village assets. If a burner on your stove goes out, its nice knowing that, instead of driving twenty-five miles to a store, Joe down the street has a stove or two in his back lot. Even better is knowing that you have something Joe wants. Some dickering and a trade later, you have a burner for your stove.

When you live in the outback there is little that can't be used in one fashion or another, and there is room to store the good junk. But since urbanites and suburbanites have moved into the village, junk has been devalued. Nowadays our junk has been finding its way to the urban landfill.

ooo

A long time ago, a pair of professionals moved into the village in a house that overlooked a small field full of good junk. Much of the junk was automotive and was a good source of vehicular odds and ends. I got a number of good parts for an old Chevy I was working on, and I know that many village people appreciated the industry it took my friend to gather that much good junk.

The professionals had been in their house for several months when out of the blue my collector friend was served with a complaint from the county. It seems that he had an overabundance of vehicles on his property.

The complaint had been submitted anonymously but the consensus was that the new folks had blown the whistle. Boy, did that piss everyone off. The village had lost a valuable resource. The village drums told the story and soon the newbies were getting the collective glare.

The woman of the professional pair, a very smart and savvy woman, made it clear, at the post office and the store, that her husband was not the one who made the complaint. The pressure lifted from the newbies and the issue faded into history.

But the story is not over; it gets rich with the warmth of human cleverness. About a year later, the rumor drifted around the village that the woman was telling the truth, the husband had not made the complaint — she had. I love it.

That family has survived. Muy savvy. The field is still full of good junk, but it's been organized into more respectable-looking piles. The professionals realized they had pushed the wrong button, in the wrong way, if they wanted to live here.

The professionals endured and have contributed valuable input in the various battles the village has faced. The truth is that the village doesn't mind a good argument and appreciates clever rhetoric. Also, most of us have learned to take rumor with a large dose of salt.

ooo

The move against junk can be very disruptive to village life. We've had example after example of people who moved here and then tried to clean us up, an attempt that is often absurd. For example, one couple built their house, moved in, and immediately began to complain about the junk in a nearby yard and alleyway. Indeed, one member of the new couple gathered and discarded some of the neighbors' junk, stuff that was in the common alley.

The village drums beat hard. There was some heavy dialectic. One theme was that common property should not be used to store personal junk. Another theme was that the couple knew what they moved next to. How dare they now act like they had been violated?

The incident was allowed to pass over, and the couple have become accepted members of the community. But the incident represented one more inroad against junk.

ooo

The issue of junk came to a head several years ago when someone filed a complaint against one of the biggest, if not the best, patches of junk in the village. The family has been collecting for several generations and has some really nice stuff, quite diverse: cars, refrigerators, trailers, miscellaneous artifacts. No one knows who blew the whistle, but the subsequent shootout became the stuff of village legend.

The owner of all the fabulous junk went on the offensive with powerful discourse. First there was a four-by-eight sign posted at the front of the property, telling everyone what for. The discourse continued in the form of complaints lodged against everyone in the village who was in violation of any county ordinance: too many dogs, too many cars, construction without permits. You name it, it was pointed to.

The poor county compliance officer soon found that life is not simple in the village. The compliance officer issued some minor change orders, the sign came down, and the complaints against everyone else were dropped. And everyone lived happily ever after.

ooo

But the dialectic continues. A friend of mine had an old truck in his back yard, a valuable piece of junk that had contributed parts to numerous other old trucks. It had been picked to pieces and was ready to be thrown away. To get it out of his back yard, my friend had to take down a fence and roll the truck out down the hill, which he did.

He parked the remnant of the truck on a lower street and called for a tow service to pick it up. It took the tow service a while to get to the task. In the meantime, all hell broke out.

Two people who had in the past been accused of harboring too much junk got exercised over the derelict pickup. They called the owner of the truck and, unsatisfied with his response, talked with a member of the local advisory council.

This incident over junk went away as soon as the truck was finally towed, but it illustrates the ongoing attack against junk. I've thought a lot about the junk issue and come to the conclusion that, unless it poses a health threat, junk should be guarded. Maybe not for newcomers. Maybe they should have to live by the rules they want. But the old farts should be allowed to keep what they've garnered through their labors.

My sentiment overlooks aesthetics in favor of pragmatism. As the world becomes increasingly aware of the need to conserve, processing every resource seems like a wise course.

My sentiment does not rule. As newbies roll into the village, the junk has been moving out. Soon we could be as clean and sterile as one of those suburban gated communities where you can't park a car in front of your house, much less work on one in your driveway.

As I've watched the junk move out of the village, I've also watched a diminishment in human relationships. First, there is division between those who do and those who do not appreciate junk. Second, there is a diminishment of trade within the village. Most people now just go into town to a store and deal with people who could not care less about human interaction and the equality of barter. The village is slipping away before my eyes.

ooo

Junk was not a problem for early settlers. Something thrown away by one person would be coveted by another. The little bit of waste that was not usable was generally taken over the hill and dumped in a ravine, a solution that worked for many years. The only lasting residential junk that I've seen in my travels through Nevada's old settlements has been in ravines used as dumps for excess paper, cans, and bottles. The old dumps are getting picked through so that what is left in them is well-broken-down paper products, broken glass, and shells from target practice aimed at all those bottles and cans.

Attitudes toward junk have changed, and more good stuff is ending up in landfills. The toxicity of junk has also changed.

After forty years of use, the village dump became dangerous. Leaking barrels of strange liquids began to show up.

A village family ran a delivery system for garbage, but the dump was made available to everyone. The dump had a gate fastened by a chain made up of one large chain, linked together by locks owned by various village residents. But the locks on the gate did not stop the covert dumping of suspect materials.

Cecil, the fox, has been the environmental sheriff in the village for many years. He berated people for changing their oil in the dirt alleys long before such practice became illegal. Cecil was worried about the barrels of leaking fluids. He called the health district and various other official bodies and ended up making some village enemies. It was just so easy to drain that oil in the alley. The solution mandated by the county was for us to become part of the urban solution; we are now contributing to the vast landfill that serves two million people.

The difference in scale is important. The Old West village system of waste disposal is hardly adequate for a population of two million people, particularly when those people can't be bothered to pick through and thin their own garbage. The old and easy notion of simply taking the junk over the hill is not a viable solution.

The problem is not just that people are throwing away a lot more stuff; the stuff is getting bigger. It is not uncommon for an urban center to eliminate whole neighborhoods in an attempt to renovate a neighborhood. In Las Vegas it is nothing to knock down a complete, functioning hotel-casino in order to build a bigger and better version.

We know we should recycle our waste and put it to good use. That is common sense and environmentally fair. But contemporary landfills remain the cheap way to get rid of our waste. We are not addressing the question of how to best transform our waste to valuable products.

We know how to process waste, but it's a labor-intensive process. The village tends to respect the usable aspect of junk and on garbage day we take a look at what our neighbors are throwing away. But most of our garbage is going away, to the other side of a big hill, out of sight and out of mind.

Junk is an issue everywhere. The old solutions do not work on a large scale, and new solutions have not been able to economically compete with the easy devastation of yet another beautiful valley buried in garbage.

I'm not sure how we solve the junk problem. In a small setting like the village, we can trade, barter, and give away a lot of our good junk to a neighbor. We can use our grass and tree clippings as mulch and compost. If we still had some livestock, we could use our kitchen waste for animal feed. These are not options for people who don't know their neighbors, for people living too close for farm activities. Nor are they options for a village living under urban rule.

ooo

I would like to reopen the village dump and go back to the days when people had to deal with their own waste. Someone would have to live at the dump to keep it orderly, clean, and processed. Everyone would have to pay a dump fee based on the costs of processing garbage to usable material. I'd also like to get some chickens, goats, sheep, and pigs in the village. I don't think I am likely to get my way.

If I had my way, I also would decentralize urban dumps and make them more proximate, more visible, clearly a concern for everyone. My urban and suburban dumps would have an owner who lived on dump property and would be paid by fees that would cover the processing and aesthetics of garbage disposal.

When almost everything was considered a treasure, the old-fashioned landfill was a resource. But scale and centralization have turned the landfill into a significant environmental scar.

A centralized urban/suburban/rural dump system could work if funded well enough to process the incoming waste of millions of people. Turning the dump into a factory may be the solution of the future. In the meantime, the village and the adjacent suburban and urban neighbors are hiding their junk on the other side of a tall hill.

The village solution to junk can work in small rural settings. But most rural areas, at least in Nevada, have been pushed into the same laws and standards mandated by the urbanization of waste. The situation is rich in irony. The village solution that has worked in rural areas has been outlawed, but the village solution is essentially the same solution used by urban centers where the rural model does not work.

Law Enforcement

Law enforcement is a major concern in large urban units. Several years ago, a California city experienced a bank robbery in which the bad guys had better firepower than the constabulary. As a consequence of evolving, organized, and terrorist crime, urban law enforcement agencies have become more like armies than domestic peacekeepers. The size, organization, and remoteness of urban law enforcement are alien to the village.

In the American Southwest, village law was often in the hands of village citizens. I suspect that in all communities, some aspects of the law are dealt with on a citizen level. This is not always a good thing. Western literature is redundant with stories of local justice gone awry, of hangings not deserved.

According to local legend, my village has had one hanging. I have never found any documentation verifying this, but I have seen and been a part of citizen peacekeeping.

ooo

When we first moved to the village, the drums were still telling the story of villagers taking the law into their own hands. One of the village kids had fallen into an unused, deserted mine shaft. The police had arrived on the scene but were moving slowly. The boy's parents were filled with fear; the village was pumped with the need for action. And the village had better talent for a mine rescue than the officers from town.

There was a brief but intense confrontation between the officers and villagers. As I understand the story, more than twenty big men showed up at the mine shaft with all the equipment necessary to attempt a rescue. The cops did the reasonable thing and turned the task over to the locals.

As it turned out, the village lost a son, another victim of mining laws fabricated by commercial interests, laws that fail to protect the innocent. But the horrible event demonstrated how the law can be taken into the hands of the villagers, the people who give life to a village.

There are pros and cons and numerous consequences to citizens taking the law into their own hands. Sometimes such action is applauded. A year or so ago, I read a newspaper story about an elderly woman who, in the course of a home robbery, shot several of her attackers and ran the remaining bad guys down the street. It seems like everyone liked that story.

ooo

In the village we have lots of guns. We are Americans. We try not to use them on one another. One man in particular had a great arsenal, and he knew how to use it. We called him "the sheriff."

The sheriff was an Old West hybrid, one of those men who bridged the generation between cowboys and truckers. He was a big man, favored Western shirts, boots, and a cowboy hat, and drove the big rigs. He gave John Wayne a good run on the rugged Western look.

We appropriated an old sheriff's sign and hung it on the village market. Our sheriff often could be found sitting on the store porch, under the sign, looking the part. Touroids often took him for the sheriff; sometimes we took him as our sheriff. He was a residual of the Old West and was not afraid to defend himself, his family, and his friends.

And so it was that one day strangers backed a truck into a village garage. The word went out that it looked like there was a burglary going on. When the truck and its two occupants drove away, they had to swing by the sheriff's home. He stood in the middle of the road with his right hand slightly behind his back. They stopped, he stepped up to the driver's window and laid the barrel of one of his biggest pistols on the window sill. He had some big guns.

You can imagine the conversation that ensued. "What are you boys up to?" That's how I imagine our sheriff starting the conversation — he was a direct sort of man.

It turns out the alleged burglars had been paid by the owner to move some materials from the garage. The sheriff let them go. I hate to think of some of the potential downsides to the sheriff's action. But then again, you need to consider the context. At the time of the alleged burglary, the village was an hour away from police response.

ooo

Villagers have traditionally policed themselves. Many years ago, one young village bull thought that another young bull was trying to mess with his mate. He didn't like that. One night the mated bull charged up to the Tree Bar and proceeded to nail the young bull with a powerful right. Vigilantes dragged them apart and sent the married bull home.

But he wasn't done. He roamed the edge of the herd, and bellowed a strong challenge to the young bull. The married bull was a big boy, weighed in somewhere around two hundred pounds, and had worked in law enforcement. Like a herd, our ears went up, and we listened.

One of our 350-pound miners, a real teddy bear, one of the nicest men I've ever known, went out into the night to talk the big bull down. The big bull made the mistake of striking out at the miner, who then picked him up by the elbows, laid him on the ground, and told him that he would let him up but he had to go home and cool off. And he did.

I know that community policing can get ugly. For example, the case down in Texas, in a small town that had a man who had everyone scared unto death. One day, half the town showed up with guns and blew the bad guy into oblivion. No witnesses ever came forward, and no one was prosecuted for the community-enacted death penalty. Fortunately, we have not had such an extreme situation in my village.

ooo

We remain vigilant but we now have a formal constabulary. We are under the jurisdiction of a metropolitan police force. Formal response time has improved, and the urban police unit now has helicopters. Village response to criminal activities has become less forceful and more informational.

Not too many years ago a man drove through the village trying to pick up young children. Our kids are generally advised to be cautious of aliens and, when approached by one, they run. One of the kids ran to the Tree Bar and other kids ran home, to the post office, or to the store. Within minutes, the whole village was on its collective toes, and the police had been called.

We started following the stranger, tag-teaming him from one street to another. We called in his license plate number, which turned out to belong to a pedophile. We made no attempt at contact. Twenty minutes from the first contact with our children, the stranger was in custody.

ooo

Villages traditionally have a constabulary, a body of constables who keep the peace and settle disputes that can be resolved on the spot rather than in a courtroom. My village has moved from the Old West to modern law enforcement.

In the cowboy days, the primary constable was the sheriff, who packed a .45 on his hip, was hard as nails, and could go all day on one bite of jerky. But many moons ago, the urban and rural law enforcement personnel were rolled into one unit.

The sheriff is elected and so he is an urban choice. Fortunately for the village, the sheriff assigns sergeants to the outlying areas. Those sergeants have been a mixed bag. Sometimes they take an active interest in what the village is all about and make sure their officers follow a policy that works with the local community.

Sometimes the urban law enforcement brain comes to the conclusion that close community relationships can lead to corruption. Movies have been made about how local contact can subvert the best of men. Once in a while, we've ended up with an incredible mismatch of officers and village folks.

My favorite mismatched officer earned a particularly unflattering nickname. Twitchy was a sensitive, honest young cop. When he was assigned to us, he had no idea what hell he was going to go through. My first contact with him came during the Tree Bar war.

One Saturday night when the music had been particularly loud, an irate woman called the constabulary. The constable was late but he took a verbal report. He didn't know us; as far as he knew, we were a bunch of yahoos disturbing the peace with our drunken party.

The next Saturday night, he stopped by the Tree Bar. He received a "good evening" from everyone and the music stopped. Now, he could have said that he was just visiting, taken a seat, and popped a Pepsi. But no, he had to make it hard.

He whipped out his flashlight, which was much brighter than the lantern used at the Tree Bar, and spotted each of the fifteen or so people sitting around, enjoying the music. After he had spotted everyone, he focused his beam on the floor.

"What are you looking for?" one village wit asked.

"What do you think I'm looking for?" Twitchy asked.

The Wit took a moment to think about it, and then said, "Your shoes?"

Twitchy didn't like that.

So he took to watching us in the early afternoon, when the miners would get off work, and people would meet at the Tree Bar for a few beers.

The Wit also happened to be the man who took care of the sprinkler system. He set one of the large, timed sprinkler heads to face the street instead of the park. One afternoon while Twitchy was watching us from the high road, the Wit walked over to the pump house and turned on the timer.

He walked back to the Tree Bar, sat down, and said, "This should be good."

We didn't know what he was talking about until the sprinkler system came on, and the Wit pointed to Twitchy's vehicle, which was, at that moment, getting a good douche. Unfortunately for its occupant, the vehicle's windows were open.

Swish, swish, swish. The spray went past the vehicle. And then, pst, pst, pst, the sprinkler returned to once again water the inside of Twitchy's official vehicle.

Have I explained why Twitchy is so called? He has an unseeming and involuntary response to irritation of any sort — his eye twitches. Lamentably, we live in an irritating world.

We live in a particularly hard world for our Twitchies. They can't go to the beach because they probably will see someone drinking or smoking what they should not be drinking or smoking.

The Twitchies of the world believe the law, to the letter of the law. The world at large is incredibly lawless. From the president on down, the political structure seems incredibly corrupt. For our Twitchy, drinking in our park seemed like a kind of corruption.

Twitchy left us for a more outlying area, but then he came back. He seems more relaxed and more willing to patiently sort out the occasional calls he gets from the village. He once showed me an incredible act of compassion. But not before he patrolled an area much further out than the village, in the last of the old, desolate West.

ooo

I don't know if this is true — it came to me through the village drums, which can be remarkably creative and fictional. I heard that Twitchy didn't have much good luck in the outlying areas. The outlying areas are generally populated by outlying people, people who need some distance for any number of reasons. Such people do not relish a close relationship with the constabulary.

The rumor is that Twitchy was invading some personal spaces. The next thing you know, he was driving through the desert one lonely, dark night and shots were fired over the hood of his vehicle. He could honestly say that his vehicle had taken both fire and water.

The story has it that Twitchy called headquarters, and The Force arrived. As I heard the story, there were helicopters, dogs, assault vehicles and scores of officers on the site of the shooting before an hour had passed.

Nary a track could be found, nary a shell. Twitchy was twitching.

Here's the sad part. I think everyone takes the twitchy eye as a sign of impending violent, irrational, all-out action. No, it was just a tell of agitation. In all of my various dealings with Twitchy, I never saw him engage in precipitous action. Oh, if things got hot, he'd put his hand on his gun, but I count those as valuable tells and try to act accordingly.

ooo

Twitchy is still alive and here. He is very discreet and gentle with village problems. We had a young runaway in the village who tried to commit suicide in the village park. He made a bad job of it and bled his way to the surrounding desert. The blood trail was called in, we started the search, and we found the teenager under a mesquite tree, bleeding out his life.

Twitchy could have been a hard-ass but asked no hard questions. He took over the scene, brought medical backup, and consoled the teen as best he could. He brought compassion to the scene. He doesn't live here, but he's become part of the village.

ooo

For the past many years, the village has been blessed with really nice leadership and fieldwork by its constabulary. Our sergeant comes to many of our community meetings, and he has a good understanding of community standards. What he knows is there are some laws that a community does not follow. Not following the law can take many forms.

We once had a young officer who gave parking tickets to people facing the wrong way on the street in front of the post office. For as long as anyone could remember, people had parked every which way in the village and there never had been any problems.

For some constables, all laws are absolute. For village constables, there is a deeper understanding of human complexities. You deal with the tough stuff first. You don't bother looking at the small stuff. Or, if you do see something you should not, as an officer of the law, you handle the situation like a human being.

ooo

A long time ago, a man in the village had some magnificent pot plants, eighteen feet tall, in his back yard. They looked like pine trees. One afternoon, the constable parked his vehicle a block away from the back yard and walked to the back door of the grower. He knocked. When the door opened he pointed to the plants and said, "I can't be seeing this." And he walked back to his vehicle. The next day the plants were gone, and never reappeared.

ooo

My favorite constables were as close as brothers. They both made an effort to know their territory, and they are both marvelous people. When they came to the village, they were toward the end of their constabulary careers and smart as whips.

My first sight of Bullet, as I call him, came while I was at the Tree Bar, when he pulled up to the market and got out of his large police SUV. His head was shaved (as shiny as a bullet), and he was built like a linebacker. I didn't like him at first sight. He also walked with a swagger. He reminded me some of the cocky roosters back at the ranch.

My first contact with Bullet was adversarial. One of the kids ran up to the Tree Bar and told us that one of our villagers, the Wit, was being busted. We knew that he was having legal problems and thought we might be able to help explain matters to the constabulary. We also knew the Wit could be a pistol to deal with and thought we could be of some help to the constabulary.

A bunch of us got in and on my truck and zoomed to the rescue. When we arrived at the scene, Bullet had the Wit in deep conversation. We piled out of the truck and Bullet stepped forward and ordered everyone to stop at once, which we did.

I stepped forward and started to explain the situation, and then Bullet had me draped over the hood of my truck. Holy moly! He was fast. He noticed an empty beer can in the truck and wanted to know if I had been drinking.

A beer or two, I told him, and he ran me through some sobriety tests. Having spanked me in front of my friends and neighbors, he ordered us back into the truck and on our way.

After I licked my bruised ego and thought about the matter, I realized that Mr. Bullet had handled the situation perfectly. He didn't need help.

A few days later, I saw Bullet in the store and asked if I had passed the test.

"What test?" he asked.

"Why, all the standing on one foot and reciting my numbers backwards. How'd I do?

"Oh, you passed," he said. "Barely."

"Will I be getting my diploma in the mail?" I asked.

"No," he said, "we throw the small fry out."

The next Saturday night, Bullet and his partner, Smooth, showed up for music in the park. They drove up in their black-and-white, walked into the Tree Bar, said hello to everyone, took a seat, and popped some soft drinks. The music played on, and our new constables made themselves part of the community.

They became honorary members of the village. They came to many of our meetings, they introduced themselves to people in the village, and they occasionally would hang out at the store. They had their retirement party in our community hall. They had half the police force and a good number of the villagers on hand for the party, and everyone had a good time.

ooo

After our two best-ever constables retired, we got a new resident constable, about forty years old, an experienced and dedicated peacekeeper. He had checked us out, liked what he saw, and bought a home here. He, his wife, and children settled into village life.

Our resident was a quiet sort who showed up at village meetings and parties but never said too much. It became clear that he walked a fine line between his affection for us and his duty to the law. Everyone respected that and no one rubbed his nose in blatant abuses of the law.

One day at the Tree Bar, we noticed a big floater Cadillac pull into the village. The man at the wheel was big. We could hear the car slowly roll through the village and then he came back into sight.

He stopped at a group of children and engaged them in some conversation. This is always a warning sign for us — strangers talking to our children.

One of us started walking toward the car and it drove off. A call was made to our new resident cop, who said he could be in the village in about ten minutes. In the meantime, the alien stopped at another group of kids and started a conversation.

At this point we mobilized. We got into our various vehicles and drove around in an apparent random fashion while making sure that someone was always in sight of the Cadillac. The man pulled into the southwest corner of our baseball field, got out of his car, and went to sit on the bleachers. One group of villagers settled into the southeast part of the field and another group gathered at the northwest corner. It looked like just another day in the park. But in this case, all eyes were on the drama at the bleachers.

Our resident cop drove up, got out, and walked over to the man. We could not hear what was being said but we presumed that our resident was explaining that a call had been made and that he was just checking things out. The man got up from his seat and stood over our resident in an obviously belligerent fashion.

The man had about eighty pounds on our resident, who did not look imposing on first glance — he was of medium height and build. But if you looked closely you could see that he was in perfect condition. He would bicycle twenty-six miles as a minor morning workout.

Anyway, the man thought he was dominating the situation, and that's the way it looked from the distance of a hundred yards. And then the man's coat came loose and everyone could see a pistol at his side. Uh oh.

What happened next happened so fast that I can only report a general impression. One minute the man was leaning over our resident with his hand hanging down by his gun. The next minute, the officer had the man in a headlock with a pistol at his ear. The man was cuffed, checked out, and found to be an ex-felon with outstanding warrants. He was taken off the streets.

Our resident didn't go around looking for trouble, but he certainly knew how to handle it when it came his way. He was Socrates' man of silver, a good watchdog of the state who handled residents with decency and gentleness but could be ferocious when ferocity was required.

ooo

We lost our resident in a horrible fashion. He was the victim of a hit-and-run. The family, the village, and the police force were all devastated.

In megalopolis, the constabulary tend to be remote and often feared action figures. In a village with resident peace officers, there is an interpersonal relationship between the officers and the villagers.

My village has attained a nice relationship between village and official law enforcement. Our constables are respected and our community standards are respected. We don't do the heavy lifting, the apprehension, but we are witnesses and formularies in the process of law enforcement. I don't think the same can be said about megalopolis, where people see nothing.

Queers

To listen to some Taliban Christians, queers will lead to the end of human civilization. In the village, we've found that queers are just another interesting human manifestation.

When I was a kid on the ranch, the word "queer" meant something odd. One time I was raising chickens for a 4-H program and the chickens started disappearing. There were no holes dug under the fencing and no tracks of marauding varmints like skunks, coyotes, or bobcats. The situation was queer. So was the truth of the matter, when we finally ran it down.

We also had a few pigs at the time, in the same yard as the chickens. I started hanging around after feeding the stock and the case of the disappearing chickens was solved. I'd feed the pigs and the chickens would jump into the pig trough and eat pig food. Then one of the pigs would nail a chicken and eat chicken food. I thought that was kind of queer.

In thinking back on the matter, I realize there were homosexuals in the back country but, if the couple was female, they were viewed as a couple of spinsters. If the couple was male, the community viewed them as partners in the same way that two cowboys might be partners. Or, sometimes, paired males would be viewed as a couple of "old ladies."

Sexual involvement was rarely mentioned in discussions of odd couples. Nor could any sexual involvement be deduced from the behavior of the odd couples. They were circumspect. In retrospect, I realized that the back country policy toward queerness was to neither ask nor tell.

A piece of me appreciates the old way of dealing with queerness of any sort. But another part of me questions the silence. It seems cruel that a loving couple should have to resist all outward signs of affection. It seems sad to think of someone living in a closet.

ooo

As we all know, "queer" has been replaced with specialized terminology. We now have homosexuals, lesbians, bisexuals, transsexuals, and so forth. Little by little, these various forms of queerness have become part of popular culture, known and understood by just about everyone.

Queers have been classified, itemized, and named, and they are no longer queer to most of us. Indeed, as one watches television, listens to the radio, reads newspapers and magazines, it seems like they are everywhere. Other than those people who maintain a fanatic hate for any queerness, queerness turns out to be nothing more than different.

ooo

Odd couples are present in much of village life. I suspect their acceptance derives from experiences we might all have shared. I don't mean homosexual experiences; I mean the familial, social, political, and work contacts that reveal various sexual inclinations. Most village folks have a history and came here with perspectives already in mind. I know I arrived with a preconceived notion of homosexuality.

I think I was hit on by a queer many years ago. I had been fishing. When I got back to the car, there was a shiny new sports car next to my ratty pickup. The good-looking young man noted my interest in the car and let me sit in the driver's seat. Then he whipped out some beer and whiskey, we had a few, and the next thing I knew his hand was on my knee.

I was rather drunk and only vaguely remember my escape, which was probably clumsy, inarticulate, and fast for a drunk guy. But other than this one incident, my life was essentially queerless until we moved to Las Vegas. Our neighbors were show folks and had friends from around the world and, boy, did they open our eyes.

We went to a party at our neighbors' house. They worked on the Strip and, among all the straight folks, there was an overtly queer pair that everyone accepted as just another couple. Barbara and I were fascinated.

The odd couple squabbled and argued just like any other couple. It was clear the feminine guy had been born feminine. He giggled rather than laughed. He had the languid movements of a woman. He wore women's pantsuits. It was the best show in town.

One night, our show folk friends and two of their queer friends took us to a gay bar. I was in a state of shock and made sure I didn't drink too much. I couldn't stay too long because when I had to use the restroom I realized that while the restrooms were clearly marked male and female, the clientele of each room seemed equally divided between males and females. I'd see apparent males walk into the female rest stop and females walk into the male room. It was very disorienting.

The odd couple made me realize that their sexual inclinations were actually minor relative to the depth of their relationship. They were a true couple. At first I viewed them humorously but, ultimately, they became just two people trying to make it through life, just like the rest of us.

As I've grown older, perhaps old, I've come to see queers as not really exotic. There are a lot of them running around, dealing with their particular queerness in the best fashion they can. By the time I moved to the village, I was no longer shocked by queerness. It was just a part of the human condition.

ooo

My attitude toward queerness was mostly formed when one of our best friends turned bisexual and then drifted into homosexuality. He was a scenic designer of considerable genius. He traveled around the world and tasted and tested everything.

We had known him and his wife for many years. She was a talented, beautiful woman. Then we heard through a mutual friend that he and his wife had separated and he had a boyfriend. We were shocked.

He visited us with his new boyfriend, a pretty boy with little of the intelligence we associated with our friend. Over dinner, after everyone had relaxed a little bit, the boyfriend became a person, a soft, sensitive type with no guile but a horrible disease.

I think it was 1984 when our friend was diagnosed with HIV. It about killed us. Our daughter was distraught — she loved our friend and he was an important person in her life. He visited us several times in the course of his illness. His spirit never wavered. The last time he visited he was bald from radiation treatment, and we have a picture of him with our daughter. I want to cry.

Toward the end, he was bedridden. He wife had moved in to help. Toward the very end, she tried to put him in a hospital, but he wasn't about to die in a hospital. He checked himself out, got back home, and crawled into bed.

His wife called me, and a village friend drove me into West Hollywood where my dying friend lived. I couldn't believe the deterioration. He had been a 185-pound, beautiful, talented man. Now he was down to less than hundred pounds. He had lesions on his body and was unable to move himself.

The wife was beyond her ability. So was I. I started calling medical facilities in an attempt to get some medical supervision. Everyone was afraid to walk into the apartment. I finally found a social worker with no fear. She was marvelous and very tired. She knew the disease and exactly how it progressed. She trained the wife and I in the palliatives that would make his life easier.

He died. We had a heck of a time finding a mortuary that would deal with the cremation — no one wanted to be near the body. We finally found a place that would take care of the remains.

And then we went to the address book he had instructed us to read, and called all his friends for the wake. For twenty-four straight hours, his friends poured into his apartment from around the world, straight and queer. Vast quantities of booze and drugs were consumed in the living room. Hundreds of testimonials were delivered in high style. It was a movie that remains in my mind, one that I've often replayed.

He had made a list of how his possessions and art (he was an awesome sculptor) were to be divided. As each person left the wake, he or she would take a specified possession. Eventually, the wife and I ended up in an empty apartment. We drove across the desert, to my house, with the ashes, and we walked the mountain, spreading out our loved one's ashes.

And so, we can say what we want about queerness, we can make nervous jokes, we can bluster and threaten, but the bottom line is that when it's someone you love, queerness is just another human condition.

ooo

I'd say six to seven percent of the homes in the village are occupied by queers. The village generally accepts our odd couples. Their orientations rarely rub against the orientations of others. Indeed, they are just common villagers. In village life, everyone is queer in one fashion or another, and sexual queerness, over time, has made itself at home.

Of our queer couples in the village, three are male, four are female. There are some in the village who evidence fear and loathing over our queer neighbors but on the whole our queers are just another part of the village equation.

Our most entrenched queer was raised here. Fortunately, he was a big boy. It didn't take long for most of the kids to see that he was different and they gave him the full attention that goes with any oddness. There were limits to the taunting, and this guy stuck it out in a country-western environment that could have kicked his ass. But he was a village product, and the village tolerated his oddness.

He never rubbed anybody's nose in his business. He never hit on the young. He went outside the village for companionship. He was, I suppose, in the closet. No one asked, and he never told.

Another male queer moved into the village a number of years ago with no flap at all. He was a virtual hermit. But in a village, everyone lives close and we knew his inclination. Actually it was pretty funny. He thought he was being covert, and everyone knew and couldn't care less.

We have one other male queer in the village, a man who lost his mate several years ago. He minds his own business but he doesn't make any secret of his sexual orientation. He joins in community affairs and is accepted and valued for his input in village business. Several times, his has been the voice of reason in village arguments. He is respected.

ooo

Our female queers have been more dynamic and open than our male pairings. The first lesbian moved in and went through a bisexual period where her inclinations were confusing to all of us and, I'm sure, to her as well. She eventually found a partner and everything settled down, except for some public displays of affection.

What some young people in general fail to understand is that intimate behavior is generally not acceptable in public. So this woman was in the community pool with her friend du jour, and they ended up at the side of the pool, doing some touchy-feely. The drums started talking.

The kids, of course, were fascinated. Some of them memorized the moves and could tell the story with great detail. Some of the parents were ready for a good old-fashioned tar and feathering.

I don't know if the couple heard the drums or whether they just fell into the more measured behaviors of marriage, but they settled in and have become an integral part of village life.

Our next female couple came in the form of militants. The one was on the offensive in every encounter. She backed everyone off on every subject and eventually everyone just left them alone. Unfortunately, the macho one never realized that she could have relaxed and enjoyed life. But she continued to fight everyone, everywhere, and eventually she and her partner moved. The village was relieved.

When our last two lesbians moved into the village, they were not our first homosexuals; indeed, they were latecomers. One partner of the couple used the lesbian card, hard. But in the village the card did not go far. She would meet someone and make a point of mentioning right at the get-go that she was a lesbian. Most of the men thought that was hilarious because their general response was that they, too, were lesbians: They like women.

ooo

Homosexuality is not greeted with fear and loathing in the village. Relationships are what people look for, and our fairies and dykes are well-bonded. We like that.

The village view of homosexuality has evolved beyond the knee-jerk reaction of the righteous. I ascribe the difference to enlightenment. It seems to me that the village views homosexuality as an emotional rather than spiritual issue. Some righteous zealots would have us believe that queers are spiritually bankrupt. The truth is that queers display the same levels of faith, honor, courage, integrity, and so forth found in any human being. Despite claims of spiritual origins, homophobic appeals are emotional in nature — they reside in pathos rather than ethos. We all have our physical preferences; homophobic appeals are based on a physical norm not conformed to by queerness.

In the village we are not afraid of physical differentness. A person's physical makeup is not nearly as interesting to us as a person's fidelity to union, to a person's ability to form lasting relationships based on honor, integrity, and decency.

Growth

Growth is a problem that the village shares with large urban units. The Advisory Council for the village serves somewhere around fifteen square miles. The turf includes the village, which is surrounded by a beautiful national conservation area, and some outlying private and public real estate.

The outlying private holdings are mostly two-and-a-half to ten-acre rural estates. The relationship between the village and the villas is by and large cordial. We share many economic, social, and environmental concerns. But the village and the surrounding estates have become the targets of ongoing efforts to urbanize.

There is enough vacant land in and around the village that, with a land-use or zone change, the area's population could bounce from 500 to 30,000 people. The biggest, though not the most effective, challenge came from a developer who purchased the largest private holding in the area: the mine.

The mine is up on the hill, out of sight from the village and covered by a few thousand acres ravaged by open pit mining. The new owner of the mine envisioned eight thousand homes and various commercial developments.

The new owner was undaunted by the fact that most of the mine property was composed of tunnels from mining. What had not been tunneled had been converted to pits and waste from fifty years of open pit mining. Nor was the new owner bothered by the fact that the mine did not have enough water to serve more than about four hundred houses.

Nor was he worried about the consequences of placing eight thousand houses in a peninsula surrounded by a national conservation area. Nor was he bothered that the two-lane scenic byway would not handle the traffic. Indeed, he wasn't worried about any of the true issues.

The developer wasn't worried because, I suspect, he thought he had the politics of the matter under control. I believe he felt his past and continued contributions to political campaigns would lead to the changes and services needed for his development.

Actually, he was right, he had the juice, but he was several years too late. Most of the local politicians he relied upon are now in federal prison. His national contacts have distanced themselves from his projects. But, just for a moment, he almost had his way.

As we dug into his plans, we found that he was in the process of trading pristine federal land next to the mine for ravaged mine property. Not only were our federal representatives rolling with the trade, the feds were using the same appraiser as the developer. Revelation of these facts brought things to a standstill.

Then we found that the new mine owner had made a regular practice of supplying homes, at discount prices, to his political friends. One of our younger and inexperienced county commissioners resigned when faced with the consequences of his actions. The developer lost one commission vote.

The fact-finding was arduous work and not facilitated much by the urban media. The major newspaper received a lot of revenue from the developer's advertisements. While the developer could buy two full-color ads to rant against our objections to his project, we were lucky if we could get two inches of editorial space. We didn't break through to the press until we staged two significant acts of civil disobedience.

We held a rally for the conservation area that closed the scenic byway and resulted in ten thousand signatures on a petition against the development. That got us some press.

We rented buses and brought people to the Planning Commission meeting. The commission did not like that. Toward the end of a fairly brief and acrimonious evening meeting, the chair of the commission called the police. We didn't know the police had been called until we were back on the buses and ready to pull out.

The buses had dark windows and the police, arriving on the scene from all different directions, had no idea they were running right by the people they should have been rounding up. Once they were all safely in the county building, we left. That was a fun trip.

Meanwhile, we were also working on a statewide basis, affirming state prohibitions against zone and land-use changes. This effort culminated in a public meeting where the developer attempted to persuade state legislators by filling the meeting hall with his employees, many of whom did not speak English and had no idea what the meeting was about. The developer made the mistake of having a free lunch and a mariachi band in the parking lot, so a lot of his employees gave up seats for a free lunch, some music, and T-shirts.

The T-shirts were being passed out by people who had no idea who was for and who was against the development. A lot of village folks got a shirt to wear into the meeting, and then argued against the development advertised on the shirt. In short, the state meeting turned into such a circus that most of the respectable politicians distanced themselves from the development.

The battles with this particular developer have become a part of village legend. They were a binding glue for community. The owners of the village villas contributed money for buses, signs, petition costs, and so forth. The villagers did their part. Everyone got into it; the stakes were high.

The developer ended up with only one county commissioner supporting his project. When the commissioner left office, she continued to work for the developer, an act that left quite a stink. The commissioner later went to prison.

The developer is now trying to change public mandate through the courts. The Tree Bar crew is of the opinion that it may be cheaper to buy one judge than to purchase four out of seven county commissioners.

In any event, the proposed development was quite a challenge and victory was sweet. But the challenge of development did not stop there. We had just finished our three-year battle with the developer when our federal representatives presented us with another battleground.

ooo

To the west of the village, there is a turn-of-the-century ranch that was traded to the Bureau of Land Management for inclusion in the national conservation area. The ranch sits at the mouth of one of the most spectacular canyons in the Southwest.

The federal plan for the ranch, developed through a lengthy series of public meetings, called for renovation of the historic buildings and walking paths for educational tours. The BLM let the ranch deteriorate and uses it as a junkyard for miscellaneous materials and equipment. One fine evening, our Advisory Council was presented with a proposal for development of the ranch.

The proposal was fronted by a man who had recently retired as a BLM park manager. He had a vision: a science school for grade-school kids, about fourteen thousand of them over the course of a year. The proposal ultimately called for more than $40 million in federal money for the construction of dormitories, hothouses, laundry facilities, cafeteria, observatories, and so forth.

As the plan unfolded, our consternation increased. Our main objection was water. The federal development would take a vast amount of water from the fragile desert aquifer that served several natural riparian areas and the village.

We were also concerned with the commercial overtones. The "school" was actually a concession with each student paying $150 to $200 for a three-day stay. The only feasibility report we ever received was a financial breakdown of how the concession would pay off. Not mentioned was the fact that a marvelous old ranch would be wiped off the map, and the public would not have a chance to see a really interesting piece of Southwestern history: a ranch with more than a hundred years of history.

The plans were also interesting to us because they envisioned the science school on a flood plain. We thought that was hilarious. A school devoted to desert science based on an incredible ignorance regarding its own desert space.

Our objections were generally overlooked, and the bureau went on to violate numerous federal regulations while pushing a project that could generate $44 million for the local economy. With no public hearings regarding the change in management plan, the BLM went ahead with lavish public displays of what the project would look like.

The bureau paid incredible sums for consultants, architectural drawings, and public relations. To this day, we have no idea how much money was wasted on a project that had no water and was going to be built in a flood plain.

The village, despite a great deal of human energy, did not stop the science school. Reality did the job. The entrepreneurs behind the science school had a compelling vision that included kids and science, a hard combination to argue against. The school had political support at county, state, and federal levels. But vision, money, and political juice cannot forever trump the harsh realities of the desert. Water is scarce.

ooo

Water is a major issue in the Southwest. There are twenty-five million people in five states drinking from the Colorado River. Lake Mead and Lake Powell are the primary reservoirs of the Colorado, and they are perilously low.

Village folks do not have a high regard for how the major urban centers of the Southwest have disregarded the threat of the ongoing drought. Recently, in California, 400,000 acre-feet of Colorado River water were taken from farm land and directed to urban development — more people, less food.

In Las Vegas, Colorado River water is used, treated, then returned to Lake Mead. Indeed, the large condo centers in Las Vegas are considered to be zero water users because every flush ends up back in the lake. In the meantime, a million hormones and chemicals are making their way through the treatment center and helping to create a large body of sludge that is growing larger with each passing year.

Recently, several respectable scientific organizations have come to the conclusion that, at current use, Lake Mead could be dry within twelve years. You would think such a credible prognosis would result in an instant cessation of growth.

But no, the Southern Nevada Water Authority and its masters, the Clark County Commission, continue to enlarge the water service area and base their hopes on growth. It's truly insane and, in my estimation, criminal.

The village is not linked to the Colorado River. Villagers are generally pleased that we have our own well and a collection basin large enough to sustain what we have. We tend to view the urban control of the Colorado with an admixture of humor and disgust. Unfortunately, our water is controlled by the same urban administration.

We are in the midst of a major battle with the water authority. Our well drafts from the fifty-foot level of a sixty-foot-deep well. For most of recorded history, our well has had water to the surface level; it's been a good well. Several years ago, the water level started dipping, and dropped to ten feet below ground level — that's a twenty percent dip.

The Advisory Council initiated a meeting with the water authority in an attempt to develop a plan for wise water use. The authority tends to favor plans with economic punishments for high levels of water use.

Some members of the Advisory Council, myself included, thought the better course would be to curtail excessive water use, starting with the county park. The park has five acres that the village had given to the county. Most of the park is planted in a high-water-use grass, and it takes fifteen million gallons of water each year.

The water authority told us that it had no authority over county parks. The county parks folks told us it would take several years to do the necessary studies and convert the park to low water use.

We suggested they replant with highly drought-resistant Bermuda grass that goes dormant in the winter. The representatives of the water and park authorities could not make any immediate decisions.

The water authority came back to us with a very vague plan that failed to establish a water level that would spark emergency action. The plan also failed to address the excessive water use in the county park. At the time of this writing, the water authority is advancing its still-vague plan.

In the city, golf greens are the standard. The county has economic penalties for excessive water use but the rich folks and institutions have no problem paying the price.

Homeowners, on the other hand, are encouraged to pull out all their grass, to turn their yards into concrete, artificial turf, and rocks. That doesn't work for the village. We have gardens, we have trees. We have an oasis and don't want to turn ourselves into one more asphalt icon of urbanity.

Despite the commercial and governmental pushes for growth, we've done a fair job of holding our growth to the water we have and lifestyle we want. So far, our biggest threat has come from within the village.

There is some private undeveloped acreage in and around the village, owned by speculators who want to maximize their holdings. The best way to maximize the value of real estate is through zone and land-use changes.

The Advisory Council has dealt with numerous requests for such changes, and most of the requests have been dealt with through compromise. One applicant wanted thirty-six houses on land zoned for nine dwellings. We settled on eighteen homes.

ooo

A small landholder did the most damage to the integrity of the village. When the mine laid out the village, each home had

184

an extra back lot that could be used for gardens, garages, shops, barns, and so forth. The back lots offer each homeowner the potential for personal growth and give the village a spaciousness that is priceless.

One of the first challenges to our back lot spaciousness came from a speculator who bought two houses and then tried to get the zoning changed so he could use the two back lots for an extra house. Such a change could have led to an incredible population density. The application was fought by just about everyone in the village and did not succeed.

The challenge to our zoning that did prevail came from a surprising source. The challenge succeeded with a raw, shameless, emotional appeal. A new resident, a young woman with a child who had a severe birth defect, purchased the back lot of her neighboring house, ostensibly for an orchard.

As soon as the young woman obtained the back lot, she maneuvered her way toward a zone change that would allow her to build an extra house. The village was largely opposed to her attempted change, but she used her daughter to ace her way into the change. The young woman made a visit to a new, young, female county commissioner. She brought her daughter for the visit and persuaded the commissioner that the zone change would make it possible for her to afford the medical treatments the daughter needed. The commissioner jumped to it, and before we knew what happened, the change occurred.

Fortunately, most of the other back lots were already used or held by people who had no interest in adding density to the village. But the change was made, and the suspicion is that as time goes on, there will be other houses sitting in what used to be a community with space for such things as gardening, woodworking, and storage.

The woman sold her house as soon as she sold her back lots and she then moved. The young commissioner, cute and very religious, turned out to be quite the crook. She is the same commissioner who tried to get eight thousand homes approved for the mine site. She went to federal prison. No one here mourned her imprisonment, but most people would have preferred tar and feathers.

Many of the external threats to village life have been healthy; they brought us together and made us stronger. Our internal threats have been more dangerous. The young woman who used emotional appeals to obtain a zone change also created considerable division in the village.

Vanishing Village

In reading over what I've written, I can see that at the core of my village values there is a strong phobia regarding urbanity.

Many years ago, American cities started to control the countryside. I distrust urban judgment when it touches us, which it does all too often. For example, a number of years ago, the county government decided to standardize its addresses, with numbered grids radiating from the center of town.

Under the proposed system, the village would have had addresses in the 40,000s. My address would have been something like 44,358.

Maybe folks from the city can visualize themselves as number 44,358, but we like to think of ourselves in more finite terms. I am, for example, No. 6 on my street. I can get my mind around that.

At the first meeting on the subject of address changes, the county showed up in force. Its staff just about outnumbered the audience. We heard all about the benefits of a standardized system. Being inherently distrustful of city folk, the villagers started asking hard questions. One shrewd villager wanted to know who was going to pay for the change of address on house mortgages. Another wanted to know who was going to pay for the change of address on driver's licenses. And so it went. There were no good answers. But we did schedule a follow-up meeting to give the county a chance to review village objections to the address plan.

The second meeting wasn't as dainty as the first. The planners of the standardized address plan had not considered the consequences of their plan. As a result, they could not satisfactorily answer the question of who was going to pay for it.

The audience for the second meeting was much larger than for the first, and it was unhappy. The second meeting was basically one testimony after another to the point that no one was going to change their damned address, thank you.

Our county government gave up on standardizing addresses in outlying areas. But on other issues, as I've noted throughout this narrative, urban government commonly walks over rural sensitivities and realities in ways that threaten us all.

ooo

I think it goes like this. A few people gather together for any number of reasons and create a village. Insofar as the area is rich in resources, other villages spring up and, ultimately, become contiguous enough for them to join and become a town. If enough towns become contiguous, then a city is born. Throw several cities together and you end up with a megalopolis; we end up with New York City, with Mexico City, with Tokyo, with Las Vegas.

With each step up the urban ladder, power becomes concentrated, and urban centers end up controlling nearby rural areas and turning them into resource factories. We move farther and farther away from nature. And we move farther from ourselves.

ooo

Village communication takes many forms. We talk to ourselves, we talk with close intimates, we talk in groups, and we address one another in public. In each of these forms of communication, we are in touch with one another. When we move to mass communication, in which every word is mediated, we find ourselves talking with and through machines. My machine will get back to your machine.

As we increase the number of people in our communications, we experience a greater disconnect between ourselves and our societies. I am not suggesting that the personal pronouncements of the village are inherently better than the impersonal mass communications of our urban age. What I am suggesting is that the personal characteristics of the village are necessary for civilized human society. I want the benefits of worldwide intellect, culture, history, and art found in megalopolis. As my friend Socrates might put it, I walked away from the cave, have seen the light of human culture, and have returned to the cave. I want our collective insights and visions, and I also want the personal values that originate in the village.

In reality, I think the village is being overwhelmed by the mass. Most of you are leaning on me.

ooo

My village began changing a number of years ago. The miners have left as yuppies discovered and embraced the village's rural ambiance.

One of my best friends was the first to leave. He didn't like the yuppies from the beginning. He was the man I had bid against for our first home in the village. He always had his reservations about me, but my origins were as rural as his, and we found that we shared a common ethos. One of his best gifts was his great-grandfather, who had been one of the first white men to explore and settle this area. His grandfather had five wives and fifty-some children.

A lot of people think of multiple wives in sexual terms. Not really. A wagon train would be fleeing religious persecution and, in the middle of nowhere, a man would get shot out of the saddle or nailed by an arrow or a snake, leaving a wife and four children. Do you leave them on the side of the trail to fend for themselves? Or do you pair them up with a man willing to accept the load?

Decent men accepted the burden of polygamy, and they carried through on their obligations. Their women worked hard, as did their children, settling some of the roughest country in the world.

My friend's great-grandfather was quite a character. A book has been written about him. One day he was left horseless sixty miles from the nearest settlement. He walked those sixty miles, through a hot, inhospitable desert, in narrow-toed cowboy boots.

His character, his spirit and determination, carried him through numerous physical trials. And he survived, an honorable man, surviving with mother nature and five other mothers. Sometimes I feel sorry for the poor guy.

My friend has only one wife, but he has retained the common-sense values of his great-grandfather. His first impression of the yuppies was that they had their heads up their butts. He was astounded that these newcomers could barely tie their own shoes, much less help in the work needed to keep a village going. What really irked him was that the newcomers would move here because it was so neat and then immediately try to change things.

Then there was this: A stranger, often a reporter, would show up wanting information, much like the tourist in Mexico looking for the cathedral. Invariably, one of the newest and dumbest members of the community would step to the microphone and camera. The information generally would be wrong. Sometimes the newbie would give information that really belonged in the village rather than for general consumption.

As homes have become more expensive in the village, as more and more urbanites moved here, the labor base diminished. For example, there used to be ten to twelve people who worked the park, trimming trees, working on the watering, mowing, whacking the weeds, and so forth. Now there are two people working the park.

Then another of my best village friends took off. I call him the village fox because he is one of the shrewdest people I have ever met. If he looks left, I look left. He has established another homestead, deep in the heartland of America. He is here in the cold months, but migrates out in the spring. He has established a jump point. And so it goes.

I haven't bailed, though I've thought about it. But I maintain the hope that the work ethic necessary for village maintenance has not gone away, that it's just changing form. The yuppies moving into the village are as hard-working as any miner but they are pushing paper rather than rocks. Many of them have skills and/or money that they are willing to share.

ooo

One relatively new villager is a gourmet cook. She has started an annual gourmet dinner with limited seating and expensive seven-course meals with seven different and very good wines. Some of the old-timers object to the cost of the meal and refuse to subsidize what looks like an elitist endeavor. I think they miss the point that the people who put on the dinner are working their butts off for the village. The money goes to the pool, the park, the community center.

The gourmet cook is not the only new professional to join the community. A married pair of relatively new villagers has taken over the pool's maintenance. They do a triathlon fund-raiser for the pool, they honcho the maintenance, and they have started and maintain a swim team of our kids.

I'm beginning to see more paper-pushers who are willing to engage in the physical work needed to maintain community. At our recent annual spring cleanup, thirty-three people showed up. In the course of one day we re-roofed the shower rooms, cleaned the community hall, mucked out the Tree Bar, groomed the five-acre park, and cruised through the village helping people who wanted to get rid of some of their fine junk.

It may be the case that the village is not vanishing. Maybe I am growing old, maybe I am vanishing? Or maybe the village is simply going through a transformation, going from village to exurbia.

According to Webster's, an exurb is a region "outside a city and usually beyond the suburbs, inhabited chiefly by well-to-do families." I don't know how the transformation from village to exurb will work out. I remain nervous.

It's a fragile balance. The village has new talent but also a quota of urbanites who fail to understand that the village is not maintained by tax and government. It survives on donations and personal interaction.

We also have more and more rentals, occupied by people who love the village setting and contribute nothing. And we have an urban government that constantly pushes us to expand beyond our natural resources and, ultimately, to township. Can this village survive?

ooo

I suspect that the better village sensibilities can be established in any collection of human beings. I base this belief, in part, on my excursions into Mexico and Europe. In Spain, for example, even in the large cities, I found village folks. The city neighborhoods of Spain reminded me of my village, and they came complete with a market, a neighborhood bar, a newsstand. These city villages contain a population that keeps an eye on itself, that cares about its people, that takes pride in its community.

I have found the same sense of urban village in almost every European city I have visited. But even in 1984, the year I lived in Spain, I could see that the urban village was under attack.

Large apartment and condo projects were displacing human habitat and replacing it with human warehousing.

The large American cities that I've visited contain a residual European sense of an urban village but are steadfastly moving to a more modern, warehousing philosophy. But I'm also seeing a new phenomena of development.

About forty miles from my village, there is a community being built with a mix of commercial and residential space, with small stores and markets lining the main street. Last year, according to a real estate survey, there was a strong emergence of retail town centers within the Las Vegas megalopolis. Now, according to the same survey, about forty percent of newly minted master-planned communities have a town center.

The downsizing within the urban unit looks like an example of devolution, a surrender of control to smaller units within the megalopolis. I don't know if the new urban center will make it to village standards, but the potential is there.

ooo

The village shares many of the same issues faced by megalopolis. The creation and maintenance of community, the homeless, feral children, drugs, public urination, environment, junk, queers, growth — these are the conundrums of our age. They touch us all in one way or another. How the issues are dealt with is what differentiates a village from megalopolis.

Village solutions tend to be personal and based on experience. Urban solutions tend to be remote, based more on theories and numbers than personal contact. Village life includes an appreciation of nature. Urban units tend to view nature as a commodity.

There is a powerful tension between the rural and the urban, between the village and megalopolis. Indeed, the stakes are big and we are in a war. I fear the urban disregard of nature, and I fear urban alienation. They threaten us all. I believe the village is slipping away and that we are divorcing ourselves from nature and from one another. That is a deadly combination.

I suggest that urbanites surrender before all is lost. There is still time for megalopolis to abandon its evil ways. One obvious way is "devolution." According to Webster's, devolution is "the surrender of powers to local authorities by a central government." Urban units need to surrender some of their power to village units.

The first condition of surrender should be parity in decision-making. The village should have a say in village affairs and in the use of natural resources. Any arguments regarding village affairs or natural resources should take place in a community meeting hall, up close and personal.

The second condition of surrender should be an acknowledgment that nature is not infinite any more than oil is infinite.

We can't just keep digging, burning, and defiling our natural resources. We cannot just keep growing.

Urban units need to surrender growth as the basis of human development. Years ago, when the Chinese first mandated family size, I thought it was an abomination. But now, seeing the consequences of runaway human growth, I think the Chinese were on to something.

Urban units might consider self-devolution. Urban neighborhoods can be planned for, developed, and represented in the political decision-making.

ooo

Enough about you. I see my friends heading out and I fear the loss of the village. I subscribe to newspapers of interesting-looking places but there are no secure sanctuaries. I play music here. I can go down every street and tell you who lives in each house. I can tell you their joys and their sorrows. And some of them can tell you mine. So I'm hanging in. Hunkered down with my friends and neighbors.

But I worry for us. The human herd has grown too large for the pasture. We're becoming feedlot animals. You should surrender now. Break it down to what works. Sustain rather than abuse. This may be your last chance.

Best wishes to us all.

Acknowledgments

First, I owe Barbara for having read and challenged this manuscript, many times over, over a long period of time.

Second, I owe my friends and neighbors for being such marvelous human beings.

Finally, I owe an incredible debt to Geoff Schumacher, the editor of this manuscript. He has been meticulous without being tedious, and resolute without being harsh. I feel fortunate to have experienced his thorough and thoughtful editorial scrutiny.

About the Author

Evan Blythin was ranch-raised in the outback of Arizona. He picked oranges and worked in construction while moving his way through the California community and state college system. He received his Ph.D. from the University of Colorado. A communication studies professor, he retired from the University of Nevada, Las Vegas, after thirty years of teaching, research, and service.

Blythin and his wife, Barbara, have been married for forty-three years, with more than thirty of those years spent in the village of Blue Diamond. Blythin has published numerous articles and books in his field of study. Sculpture and music have been two of his primary side interests (see www.blythinart.com).